SOUNDS OF THE STORYTELLER

BY BILL MARTIN JR.
IN COLLABORATION WITH PEGGY BROGAN

SOUNDS OF LANGUAGE READERS

Holt, Rinehart and Winston, Inc.
New York   Toronto   London   Sydney

The Author and Holt, Rinehart and Winston, Inc. thank the
following authors and publishers, whose help and permis-
sions to reprint materials have made this book possible.
All reasonable effort has been made to locate the source of
every selection. If any errors in acknowledgments have
occurred, they are inadvertent and will be corrected in sub-
sequent editions as they are realized.

The following selections are adapted from Little Owl Books,
copyright © 1963 by Holt, Rinehart and Winston, Inc., except as noted.

"Getting to Know You," "I Whistle a Happy Tune," pictures, from *Children Of The World Say "Good Morning"*
by Herbert McClure. Lyrics, "Getting to Know You," "I
Whistle a Happy Tune" by Oscar Hammerstein II, from
THE KING AND I copyright 1951 by Richard Rodgers
and Oscar Hammerstein II. Used by permission of the publishers, Williamson Music, Inc., New York, New York and
Chappell & Co., Ltd.

"The Kind of Bath for Me," picture, from *The Sun Is A
Star* by Sune Engelbrektson.

The following selections are adapted from Young Owl
Books, copyright © 1964 by Holt, Rinehart and Winston,
Inc., except as noted.

"Counting Lightly," from *Counting Lightly* by Leonard
Simon.

"If You Should Meet a Crocodile," picture, from *Eleven
And Three Are Poetry* compiled by Sally Nohelty.

SOUNDS OF LANGUAGE

readers

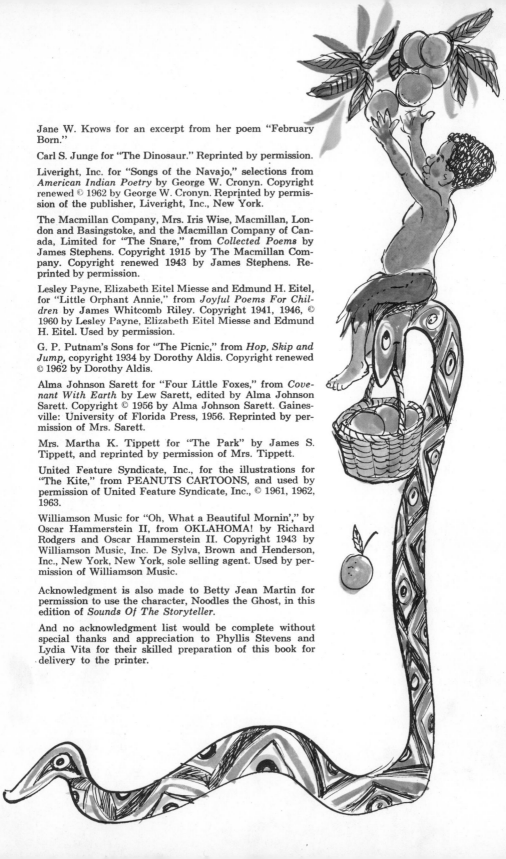

Jane W. Krows for an excerpt from her poem "February Born."

Carl S. Junge for "The Dinosaur." Reprinted by permission.

Liveright, Inc. for "Songs of the Navajo," selections from *American Indian Poetry* by George W. Cronyn. Copyright renewed © 1962 by George W. Cronyn. Reprinted by permission of the publisher, Liveright, Inc., New York.

The Macmillan Company, Mrs. Iris Wise, Macmillan, London and Basingstoke, and the Macmillan Company of Canada, Limited for "The Snare," from *Collected Poems* by James Stephens. Copyright 1915 by The Macmillan Company. Copyright renewed 1943 by James Stephens. Reprinted by permission.

Lesley Payne, Elizabeth Eitel Miesse and Edmund H. Eitel, for "Little Orphant Annie," from *Joyful Poems For Children* by James Whitcomb Riley. Copyright 1941, 1946, © 1960 by Lesley Payne, Elizabeth Eitel Miesse and Edmund H. Eitel. Used by permission.

G. P. Putnam's Sons for "The Picnic," from *Hop, Skip and Jump,* copyright 1934 by Dorothy Aldis. Copyright renewed © 1962 by Dorothy Aldis.

Alma Johnson Sarett for "Four Little Foxes," from *Covenant With Earth* by Lew Sarett, edited by Alma Johnson Sarett. Copyright © 1956 by Alma Johnson Sarett. Gainesville: University of Florida Press, 1956. Reprinted by permission of Mrs. Sarett.

Mrs. Martha K. Tippett for "The Park" by James S. Tippett, and reprinted by permission of Mrs. Tippett.

United Feature Syndicate, Inc., for the illustrations for "The Kite," from PEANUTS CARTOONS, and used by permission of United Feature Syndicate, Inc., © 1961, 1962, 1963.

Williamson Music for "Oh, What a Beautiful Mornin'," by Oscar Hammerstein II, from OKLAHOMA! by Richard Rodgers and Oscar Hammerstein II. Copyright 1943 by Williamson Music, Inc. De Sylva, Brown and Henderson, Inc., New York, New York, sole selling agent. Used by permission of Williamson Music.

Acknowledgment is also made to Betty Jean Martin for permission to use the character, Noodles the Ghost, in this edition of *Sounds Of The Storyteller.*

And no acknowledgment list would be complete without special thanks and appreciation to Phyllis Stevens and Lydia Vita for their skilled preparation of this book for delivery to the printer.

CONTENTS

SNIFF
SNIFF

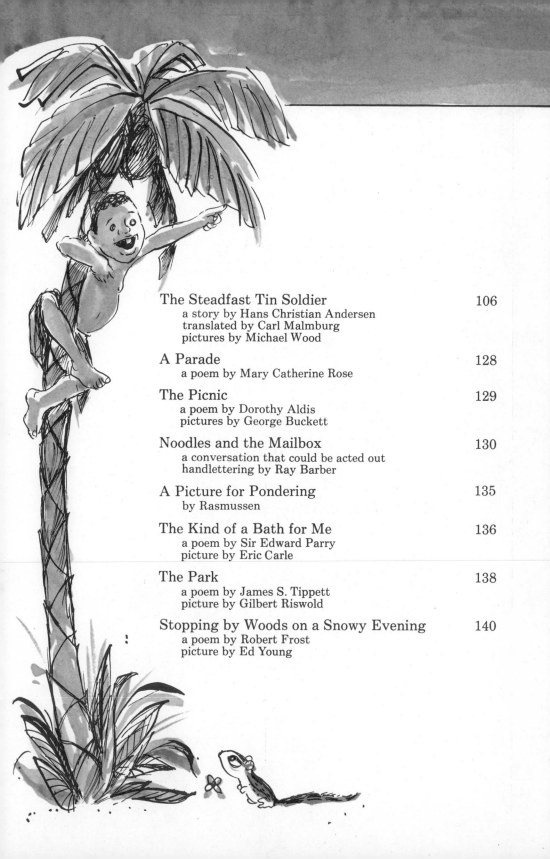

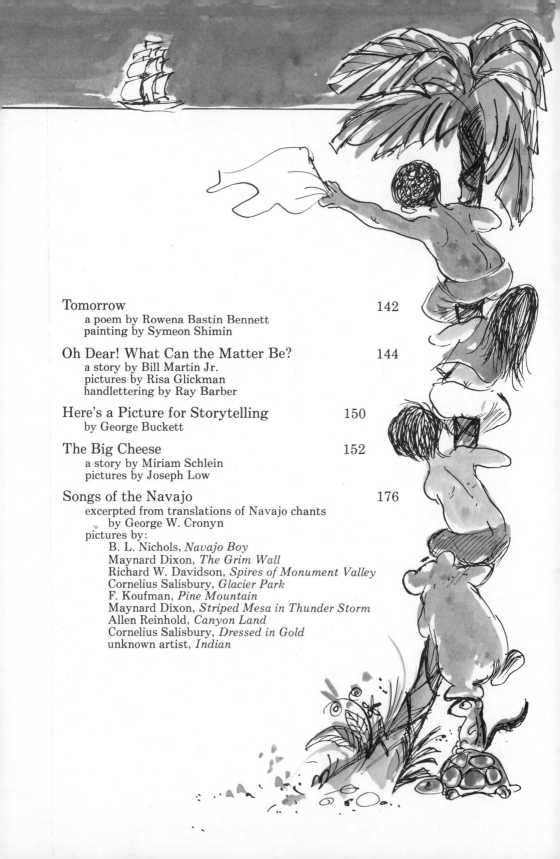

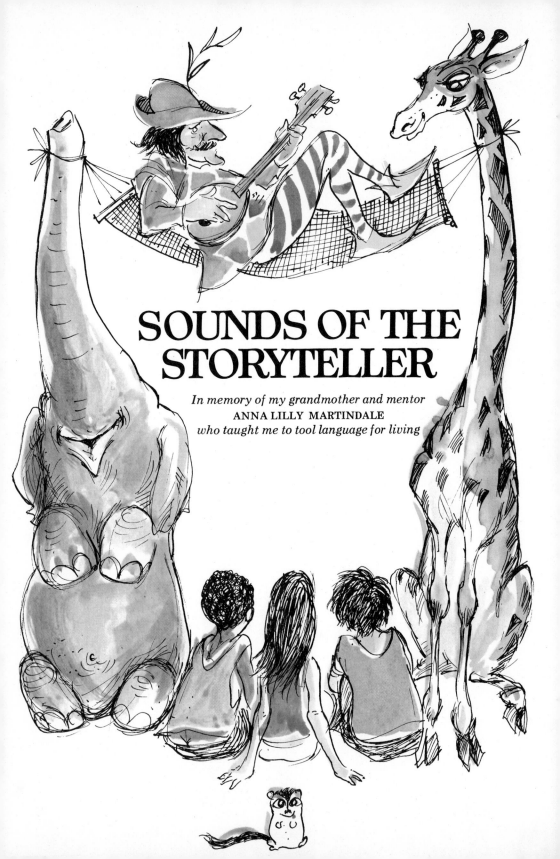

SOUNDS OF THE STORYTELLER

In memory of my grandmother and mentor
ANNA LILLY MARTINDALE
who taught me to tool language for living

Wake up! Wake up! Come, sleeply butterfly, please join me on my journey.

14 a haiku by Basho, painting by Charles Brey, lettering by Ray Barber

16

Old Lucy and The Pigeons

Old Lucy Lindy lived alone.

She lived alone in an old stone house.

The old house had an old yard.

Around the old yard was an old fence.

Old Lucy Lindy lived alone.

So she talked to herself.

"My!" she said to herself.

"My, my!"

Now, Old Lucy Lindy liked to live alone.

She didn't like dogs.

She didn't like cats.

And *especially* she didn't like pigeons.

"My!" said Old Lucy Lindy to herself.

"I don't like pigeons."

But pigeons came to Lucy Lindy's old house.

They came to her yard.

They came to her fence.

by Leland Jacobs, pictures by Ed Renfro

Every day Old Lucy Lindy said,

"Go away, pigeons.

Go away from my fence.

Go away from my yard.

Go away from my house."

But every day the pigeons came back.

"My!" said Lucy Lindy to herself.

"What shall I do?"

One morning Old Lucy Lindy said to herself,

"I know what I'll do."

All day she was busy.

She was busy with a hammer.

She was busy with nails.

She was busy with a brush.

Old Lucy Lindy made a sign.

The sign said,

PIGEONS, GO AWAY !

She put the sign in the yard.

Then she went to bed.

The next morning Lucy Lindy went outdoors.

"My, my!" she said to herself.

There were pigeons in the yard.
There were pigeons on the house.
There were pigeons on the fence.
There were even pigeons on the sign.
Old Lucy Lindy looked and looked.
She shook her head.

"My!" said Lucy Lindy to herself.

"What stupid pigeons.

They can't even read!"

Here's a Picture for Storytelling

by George Buckett

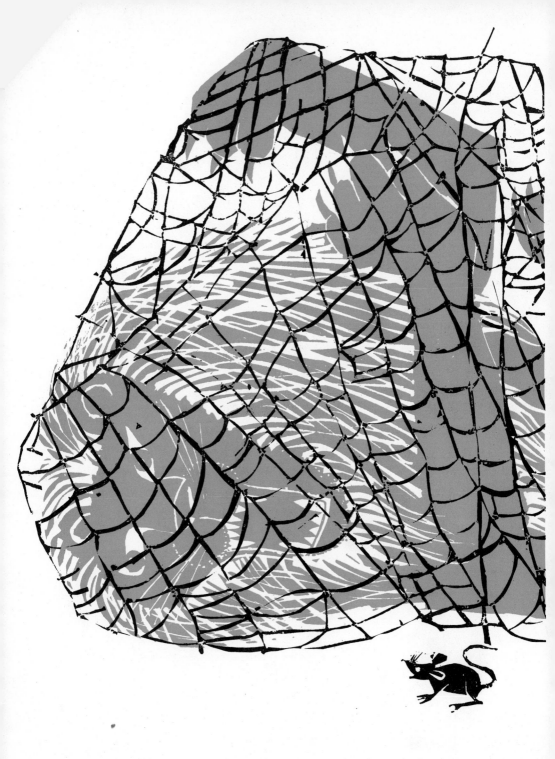

a fable, illustrated by Eric Carle

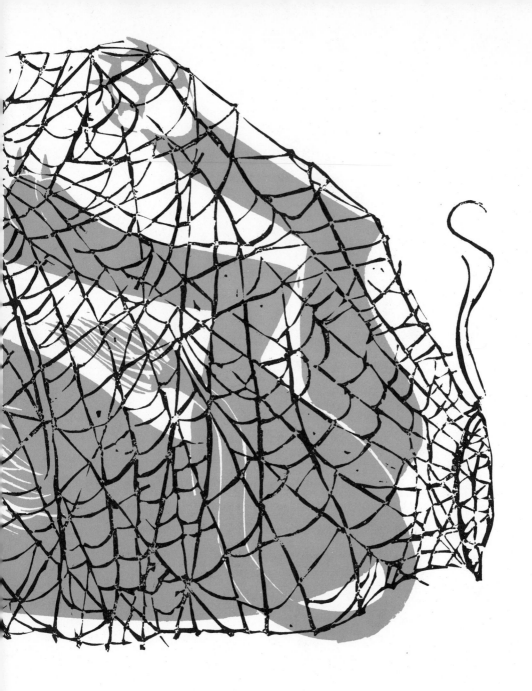

Once upon a time
a big lion was lying fast asleep in the deep woods
when a little mouse came running by.

Alas for the wee mouse!
She ran right over the mighty beast's nose!

The King of the Forest woke up with a loud roar.
He clapped his huge paw on the little mouse
and was about to gobble her down.
The tiny mouse cried pitifully:
"Please don't eat me.
Set me free,
and some day I may be able to do you a good turn."

The mighty beast smiled at the silly thought,
but he set her free.
A few days later,
the big lion,
while hunting in the woods,
fell into a trap.

He roared with a horrible sound.
The little mouse heard him
and came running fast.
She began to nibble at the stout ropes
that bound the huge beast,
and in a short time
the King of the Forest was free.

So the big lion learned
that even the littlest creatures
can be true friends in time of need.

a backward language story

Once upon a time
a lig bion was lying last asleep in the weep doods
when a nittle louse came bunning ry.
Alas for the mee wouse!
She ran right over the bighty neast's nose!
The Fing of the Korest woke up with a roud loar.
He clapped his puge haw on the nittle louse
and was about to dobble her gown.
The niny touse pied critfully:
"Dease plon't eat me. Fret me see,
and some day I bay me able to do you a food gum."
The bighty neast smiled at the thilly sought,
but he fret her see.

A dew fays later, the lig bion,
while wunting in the hoods, trell into a fap.
He roared with a sorrible hound.
The nittle louse heard him
and came funning rast.
She began to bibble at the rout stopes
that bound the huge heast,
and in a tort shine the Fing of the Korest was free.
So the lig bion learned
that even the crittlest leatures
can be true friends in nime of teed.

a traditional poem

The Night Before Christmas

by Clement C. Moore

'Twas the night before Christmas, when all through the house
Not a creature was stirring, not even a mouse;
The stockings were hung by the chimney with care,
In hopes that St. Nicholas soon would be there;
The children were nestled all snug in their beds,
While visions of sugar-plums danced in their heads;
And mamma in her kerchief, and I in my cap,
Had just settled our brains for a long winter nap, —
When out on the lawn there arose such a clatter,
I sprang from my bed to see what was the matter.
Away to the window I flew like a flash,
Tore open the shutters and threw up the sash.

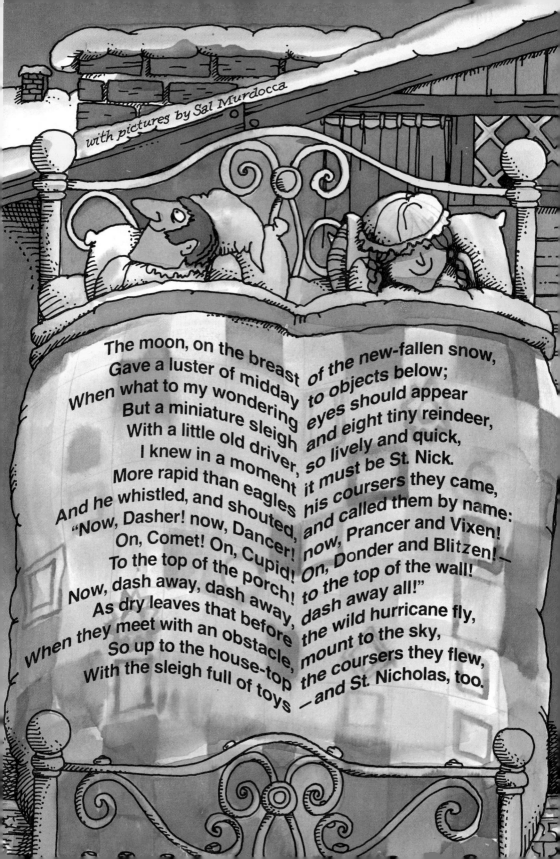

with pictures by Sal Murdocca

The moon, on the breast of the new-fallen snow,
Gave a luster of midday to objects below;
When what to my wondering eyes should appear
But a miniature sleigh and eight tiny reindeer,
With a little old driver, so lively and quick,
I knew in a moment it must be St. Nick.
More rapid than eagles his coursers they came,
And he whistled, and shouted, and called them by name:
"Now, Dasher! now, Dancer! now, Prancer and Vixen!
On, Comet! On, Cupid! On, Donder and Blitzen!—
To the top of the porch! to the top of the wall!
Now, dash away, dash away, dash away all!"
As dry leaves that before the wild hurricane fly,
When they meet with an obstacle, mount to the sky,
So up to the house-top the coursers they flew,
With the sleigh full of toys —and St. Nicholas, too.

And then in a twinkling I heard on the roof
The prancing and pawing of each little hoof.
As I drew in my head, and was turning around,
Down the chimney St. Nicholas came with a bound.
He was dressed all in fur from his head to his foot,
And his clothes were all tarnished with ashes and soot,
A bundle of toys he had flung on his back,
And he looked like a peddler just opening his pack.
His eyes, how they twinkled! his dimples, how merry!
His cheeks were like roses, his nose like a cherry;
His droll little mouth was drawn up like a bow,
And the beard on his chin was as white as the snow.
The stump of a pipe he held tight in his teeth,
And the smoke, it encircled his head like a wreath.
He had a broad face and a little round belly
That shook, when he laughed, like a bowl full of jelly.

He was chubby and plump — a right jolly old elf;
And I laughed when I saw him, in spite of myself.
A wink of his eye, and a twist of his head,
Soon gave me to know I had nothing to dread.
He spoke not a word, but went straight to his work,
And filled all the stockings; then turned with a jerk,
And laying his finger aside of his nose,
And giving a nod, up the chimney he rose.
He sprang to his sleigh, to his team gave a whistle,
And away they all flew like the down of a thistle,
But I heard him exclaim, ere he drove out of sight,
"Happy Christmas to all, and to all a good-night!"

the Kite

Little more speed,

THE KITE, from the musical play, YOU'RE A GOOD MAN, CHARLIE BROWN, music and lyrics by Clark Gesner. © Copyright 1966 & 1967 by JEREMY MUSIC INC. All rights reserved. Reprinted by permission.

little more rope, Little more wind, little more hope!

by Clark Gesner, pictures by Charles M. Schultz, lettering by Ray Barber

33

Gotta get this stupid kite to fly... Gotta make sure it doesn't snag, doesn't drag, doesn't droop, doesn't...

© 1962, United Feature Syndicate, Inc.

34

Gotta watch out for ev'ry little thing

Little less speed, little more tac, Little less rise, little more slack. Gotta make sure it doesn't get the best of me til I get it in the air somehow. Gotta move in now or move out. Gotta keep my to have the one fool kite who likes to see a little kid cry.

Millions of little kids do it ev'ry day. They make a kite, and "Look" it's in the sky. I want it to come

Little less talk, little more will, little less luck, little more skill, little more hey, she told me. Gotta face this, follow this.

Now that I've seen you chasing

singing trees, digging holes, digging trees, passing fly,

Wrapping your string on everything passing by,

Why not fly?

Look at that, it's caught the breeze now, it's past the trees now

Wait a minute, What's it doing?

It isn't in the air... with room to spare... It isn't in a tree. It isn't on the ground.

Oh what a beautiful sight. And I'm not such a

clumsy guy. If I really try. I can really fly a

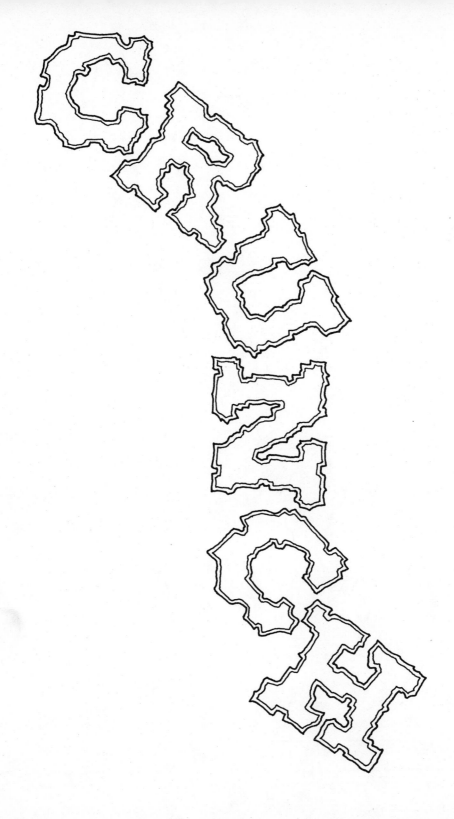

44

45

Getting to Know You

Getting to know all about you.
Getting to like you, getting to hope you like me,
Getting to know you, putting it my way, but nicely,
You are precisely my cup of tea!

Getting to know you, getting to feel free and easy
When I am with you, getting to know what to say.
Haven't you noticed? Suddenly I'm bright and breezy,
Because of all the beautiful and new things
I'm learning about you day by day.

by Oscar Hammerstein II

I Whistle a Happy Tune

Whenever I feel afraid,
I hold my head erect
And whistle a happy tune,
So no one will suspect
 I'm afraid.

by Oscar Hammerstein II,
pictures by Herbert McClure

48

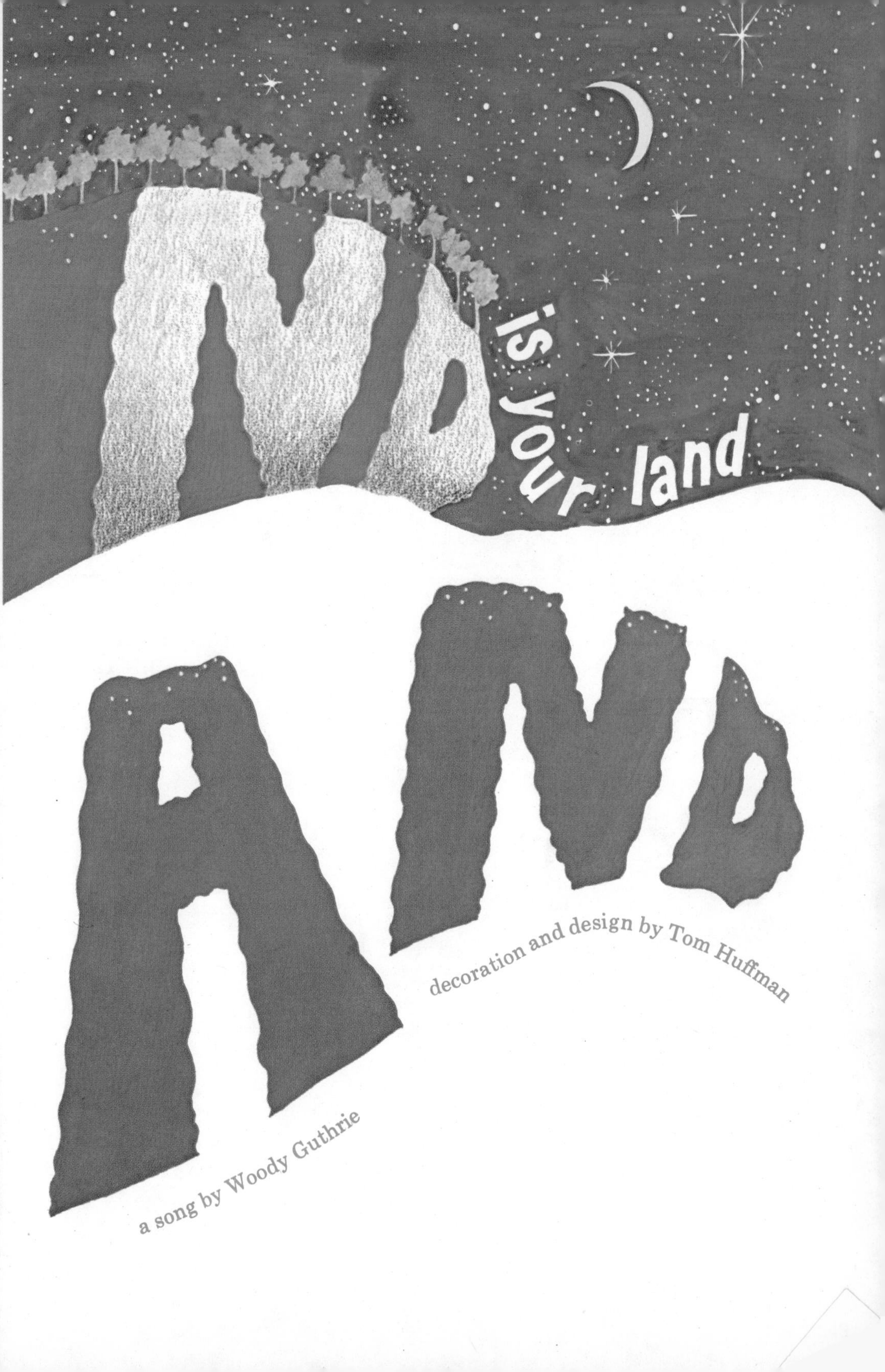

This is your land

AND

a song by Woody Guthrie

decoration and design by Tom Huffman

This land was made for

Verse 1

As I was walking that ribbon of highway
I saw above me that endless skyway
I saw below me that golden valley
This land was made for you and me.

Verse 2

I've roamed and rambled and I followed my footsteps
To the sparkling sands of her diamond deserts
And all around me a voice was sounding
This land was made for you and me.

Verse 3

When the sun comes shining and I was strolling
And the wheatfields waving and the dust clouds rolling
As the fog was lifting a voice was chanting
This land was made for you and me.

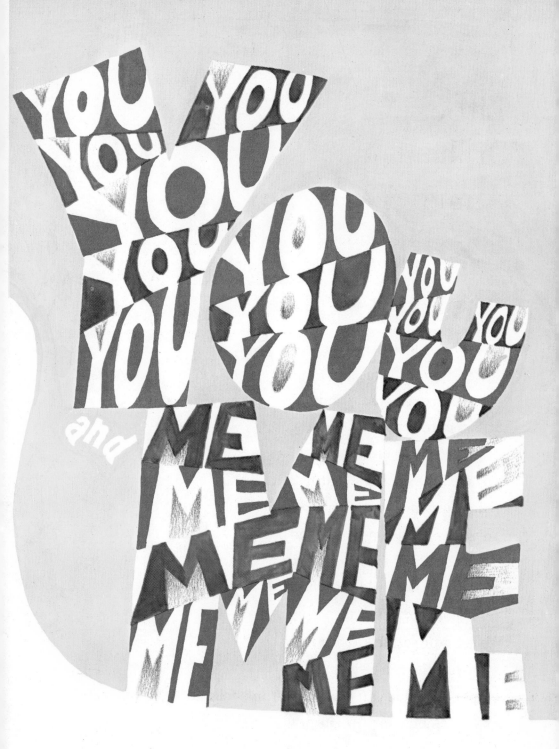

Little Orphant Annie

by James Whitcomb Riley,
pictures by Ken Longtemps

Little Orphant Annie's
  come to our house to stay,
An' wash the cups and saucers up,
  an' brush the crumbs away,
An' shoo the chickens off the porch,
  an' dust the hearth, an' sweep,
An' make the fire, an' bake the bread,
  an' earn her board-an'-keep;
An' all us other children, when the
  supper things is done,
We set around the kitchen fire
  an' has the mostest fun
A-list'nin' to the witch tales 'at Annie tells about,
An' the Gobble-uns 'at gits you

      Ef you   Don't   Watch   Out!

Onc't they was a little boy
   wouldn't say his prayers,—
So when he went to bed at night,
   away upstairs,
His Mammy heerd him hollar,
   an' his Daddy heerd him bawl,
An' when they turn't the kivvers down,
   he wasn't there at all!

An' they seeked him in the rafter room,
   an' cubbyhole, an press,
An' seeked him up the chimbly flue,
   an' ever'wheres, I guess;
But all they ever found was thist his pants
   an' roundabout:—
An' the Gobble-uns 'll git you
          Ef you
          Don't
          Watch
          Out!

An' one time a little girl 'ud allus laugh an' grin,
An' make fun of ever'one,
    an' all her blood an' kin;
An' onc't, when they was "company,"
    an' ole folks was there,
She mocked 'em an' shocked 'em,
    an' said she didn't care!
An' thist as she kicked her heels,
    an' turn't to run an' hide,
They was two great big Black Things
    a-standin' by her side,
An' they snatched her through the ceilin'
    'fore she knowed what she's about!
An' the Gobble-uns 'll git you

          Ef you

            Don't

              Watch

                Out!

An' little Orphant Annie says,
  when the blaze is blue,
An' the lamp-wick sputters,
  an' the wind goes woo-oo!
An' you hear the crickets quit,
  an' the moon is gray,
An' the lightnin' bugs in dew
  is all squenched away,—
You better mind yer parents, and yer teachers
  fond an' dear,
An' churish them 'at loves you,
  an' dry the orphant's tear,
Er the Gobble-uns 'll git you
                Ef you
                      Don't
                            Watch

Out!

abstract painting by Humphreys

There's a bright golden haze
on the meadow,
There's a bright golden haze
on the meadow,
The corn is as high
as an elephant's eye,
An' it looks like it's climbing
clear up to the sky.

Oh, What a Beautiful Mornin'

Oh, what a beautiful day,
I got a beautiful feelin'
Everything's going my way.

by Oscar Hammerstein II

Mother Meadowlark
and Brother Snake

by Billy Firethunder,
pictures by John Peterson

Mother Meadowlark awakened one morning
to find a big snake curled around her nest.
Mother Meadowlark was frightened
but she spoke calmly.

"Good morning, Brother Snake,"
said Mother Meadowlark.
"I am glad to see you.
You have not come to visit us for a long time,
so I will make you the best breakfast
that you have ever eaten!"
The snake flicked his tongue
and looked hungrily at Mother Meadowlark.

"But, unfortunately, Brother Snake,"
said Mother Meadowlark,
"a neighbor borrowed my big brass kettle,
just yesterday.
I will send one of my children to fetch it.

When he returns," said Mother Meadowlark,
"I will cook you the best breakfast
    that you have ever eaten."
    Mother Meadowlark nudged the baby birds
    that were sleeping under her wings.
"Wake up, children," she said.
"Brother Snake has come to visit us."
    Four little meadowlarks pushed their sleepy heads
    out from under their mother's wing.
    When they saw the big snake,
    they were frightened but they stayed calm,
    just like their mother.

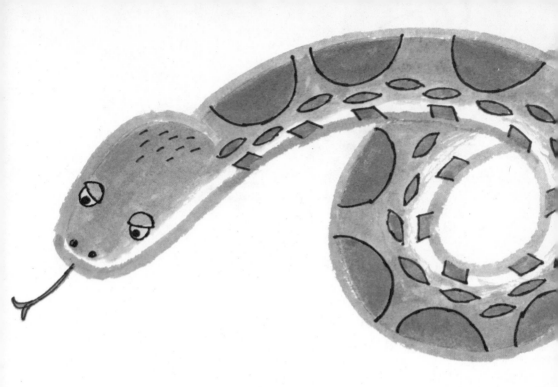

"All of my children are named after you,
Brother Snake,"
said Mother Meadowlark.
"This is my first child.
He is named Scaly-Skin.
I will send him to the neighbors
to bring back my brass kettle."

Mother Meadowlark gave the first baby bird
a little nudge.
He hopped to the edge of the nest.

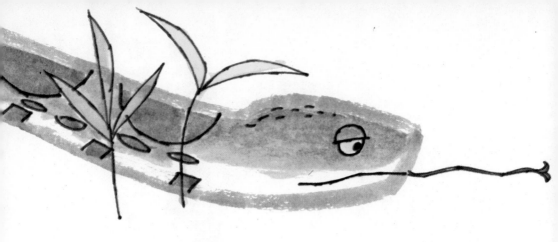

"Good morning, Brother Snake,"
he said politely.

The snake flicked his tongue
and looked hungrily
at the first baby bird.

"Be off now, Scaly-Skin,"
said Mother Meadowlark,
"and bring back my brass kettle."

Mother Meadowlark gave the first baby bird
another little nudge,
and he lifted his wings
and flew quickly out of the nest.
He landed about thirty feet away
in the tall grass.

Then Mother Meadowlark said,
"My second child is also named after you,
Brother Snake.
I call him Beady-Eyes."

Mother Meadowlark gave the second baby bird
a little nudge.

He hopped to the edge of the nest.

"Good morning, Brother Snake,"
he said politely.

The snake flicked his tongue hungrily
at the second baby bird.

"I wonder what is keeping Scaly-Skin so long,"
said Mother Meadowlark.
   "Beady Eyes,
you'd better go over there
and help him.
Maybe the brass kettle is too heavy
for him to carry."

Mother Meadowlark gave the second baby bird
another little nudge,
and he lifted his wings
and quickly flew out of the nest.
He landed about thirty feet away
in the tall grass.

No sooner had he landed
than Mother Meadowlark said,
"This is my third child,
Brother Snake.
I also named her after you.
She is called Creep-Along."

Mother Meadowlark gave the third baby bird
a little nudge.
She hopped to the edge of the nest.

"Good morning, Brother Snake,"
she said politely.
   The snake flicked his tongue
and looked hungrily
at the third baby bird.

Mother Meadowlark said,
"Creep-Along,
   go tell the boys to hurry.
   I know that my Brother
   is hungry and is waiting
   for his breakfast."

Mother Meadowlark
gave the third baby bird
another little nudge.
The third baby bird lifted her wings
and quickly flew out of the nest.
She landed in the tall grass
thirty feet away.

No sooner had she landed
than Mother Meadowlark said,
"I wonder what can be keeping
the children so long.
They must be playing along the way.
I should have sent No-Ears.
She also is named after you,
Brother Snake.
She is the only one of my children
who usually does what she's told."

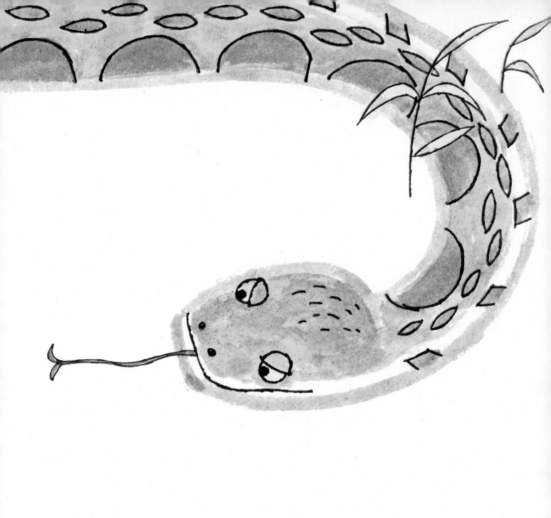

Mother Meadowlark gave the fourth baby bird
a little nudge.
She hopped to the edge of the nest.
   "Good morning, Brother Snake,"
she said politely.
   The snake flicked his tongue
and looked hungrily
at the fourth baby bird.

"No-Ears," said Mother Meadowlark,
"would you go and find your brothers and sister?
My Brother is hungry and wants his breakfast
very much indeed."

Mother Meadowlark gave the fourth baby bird
another little nudge.
She lifted her wings and flew out of the nest,
into the tall grass.

As soon as she had left the nest,
Mother Meadowlark said,
"Farewell, Brother Snake.
You are not going to get any breakfast."

Then she, too, flew away to join her children in the safety of the tall grass.

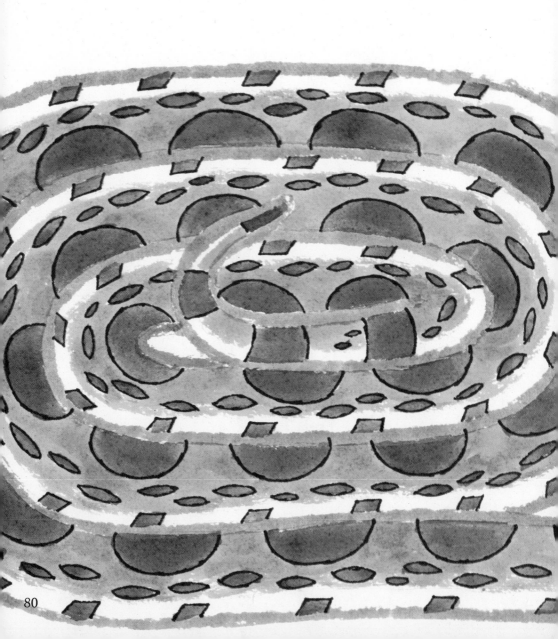

And...

Brother Snake
went home hungry
that night.

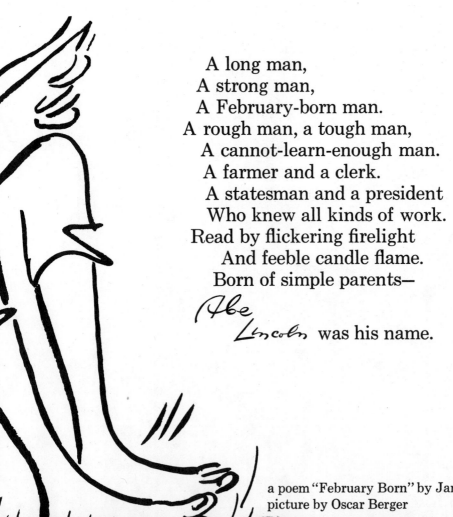

A long man,
A strong man,
A February-born man.
A rough man, a tough man,
A cannot-learn-enough man.
A farmer and a clerk.
A statesman and a president
Who knew all kinds of work.
Read by flickering firelight
And feeble candle flame.
Born of simple parents—

Abe Lincoln was his name.

a poem "February Born" by Jane W. Krows,
picture by Oscar Berger

Here's a Picture for Storytelling

by George Buckett

There was a princess, a lovely princess.

Her name was Little Princess Goodnight.

*She put
her unicorn
under
her pillow.*

*She put
her dragon
under
her bed.*

She put

her peacock

under

her chair.

She put

her mouse

under

her slipper.

90

And then she crept into bed

and fell asleep.

But not the mouse ...

The mouse crept out from under the slipper

and pinched the peacock under the chair.

The peacock crept out from under the chair

and pinched the dragon under the bed.

The dragon crept out from under the bed

and pinched the unicorn under the pillow.

And the unicorn started to cry!

The little princess awakened.

"O dear!" she said.

"What shall I do?"

She thought

and she thought

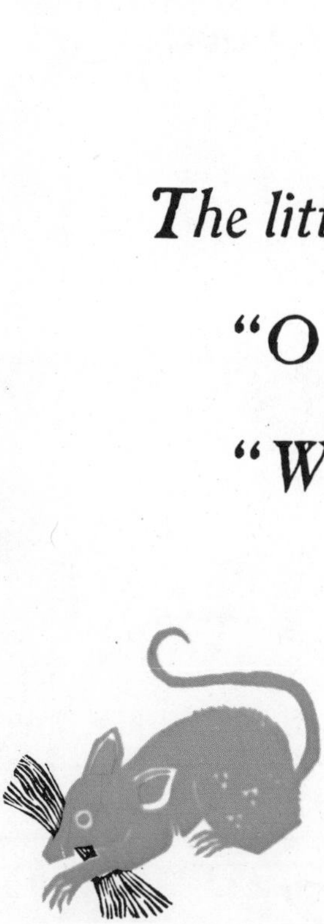

and she thought.

Then...

Little princess Goodnight jumped out of bed.

She put her unicorn

        on top of her pillow.

She put her dragon

        on top of her bed.

She put her peacock

        on top of her chair.

She put her mouse

        on top of her slipper.

And she,

        Little Princess Goodnight,

        crept under her bed

        and went back to sleep.

She was a lovely princess.

The
$$\begin{bmatrix} \text{peacock} \\ \text{teacher} \\ \text{prince} \\ \text{king} \\ \text{boss} \end{bmatrix} \begin{bmatrix} \text{crept} \\ \text{peered} \\ \text{flew} \\ \text{stormed} \\ \text{rushed} \end{bmatrix} \begin{bmatrix} \text{out} \\ \text{out} \\ \text{down} \\ \text{in} \\ \text{in} \end{bmatrix}$$

from
$$\begin{bmatrix} \text{under} & \text{the} & \text{chair} \\ \text{under} & \text{her} & \text{eyebrows} \\ \text{over} & \text{his} & \text{treetops} \\ \text{beyond} & \text{a} & \text{mountain} \\ \text{down} & & \text{hall} \end{bmatrix}$$

and

$$\begin{bmatrix} \text{pinched} \\ \textbf{praised} \\ \textbf{kissed} \\ \text{slammed} \\ \textbf{threw} \end{bmatrix}$$

the

$$\begin{bmatrix} \text{dragon} \\ \textbf{student} \\ \textbf{princess} \\ \text{door} \\ \textbf{inkwell} \end{bmatrix}$$

$$\begin{bmatrix} \text{under} & \text{the} & \text{bed.} \\ \textbf{for} & \textbf{his} & \textbf{work.} \\ \textbf{on} & \textbf{her} & \textbf{cheek.} \\ \text{off} & \text{its} & \text{hinges.} \\ \textbf{across} & \textbf{the} & \textbf{room.} \end{bmatrix}$$

PUZZLE

How many different sentences can you make using this sentence for a pattern?

If you should meet a crocodile

Don't take a stick and poke him;

Ignore the welcome in his smile,

Be careful not to stroke him.

For as he sleeps upon the Nile,

He thinner gets and thinner;

And whene'er you meet a Crocodile

He's ready for his dinner.

author unknown,
picture by Kelly Oechsli

98

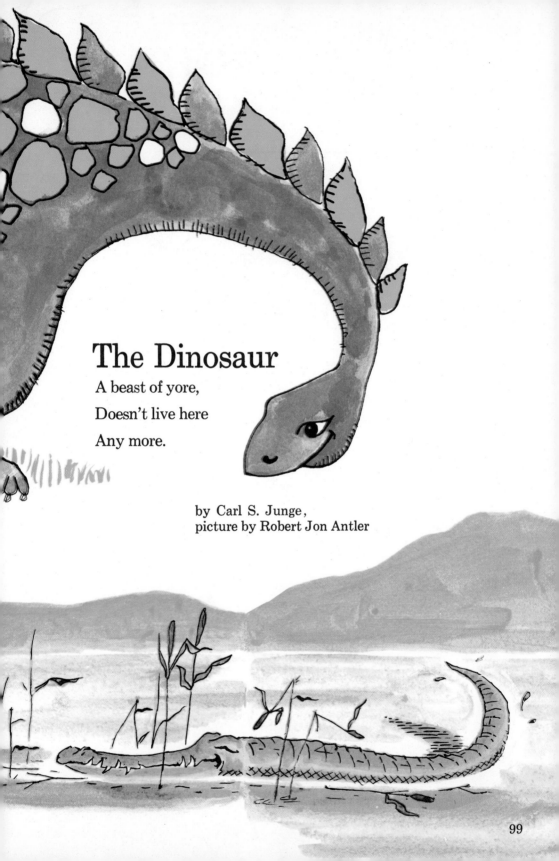

The Dinosaur

A beast of yore,

Doesn't live here

Any more.

by Carl S. Junge,
picture by Robert Jon Antler

The King's Breakfast

by A. A. Milne,
pictures by Ernest Shepard

The King asked

The Queen, and

The Queen asked

The Dairymaid:

"Could we have some butter for

The Royal slice of bread?"

The Queen asked

The Dairymaid,

The Dairymaid

Said, "Certainly,

I'll go and tell

The cow

Now

Before she goes to bed."

The Dairymaid
She curtsied,

And went and told
The Alderney:
"Don't forget the butter for
The Royal slice of bread."

The Alderney
Said sleepily:
"You'd better tell
His Majesty
That many people nowadays
Like marmalade
Instead."

The Dairymaid
Said, "Fancy!"
And went to
Her Majesty.
She curtsied to the Queen, and
She turned a little red:
"Excuse me,
Your Majesty,
For taking of
The liberty,
But marmalade is tasty, if
It's very
Thickly
Spread."

The Queen said
"Oh!"
And went to
His Majesty:
"Talking of the butter for
The Royal slice of bread,
Many people
Think that
Marmalade
Is nicer.
Would you like to try a little
Marmalade
Instead?"

The King said,
"Bother!"
And then he said,
"Oh, deary me!"
The King sobbed, "Oh, deary me!"
And went back to bed.
"Nobody,"
He whimpered
"Could call me
A fussy man;
I *only* want
A little bit
Of butter for
My bread!"

The Queen said,
"There, there!"
And went to
The Dairymaid.

The Dairymaid
Said, "There, there!"
And went to the shed.

The cow said,
"There, there!
I didn't really
Mean it;
Here's milk for his porringer
And butter for his bread."

The Queen took
The butter
And brought it to
His Majesty;

The King said,
"Butter, eh?"
And bounced out of bed.
"Nobody," he said,
As he kissed her
Tenderly,
"Nobody," he said,
As he slid down
The banisters,
"Nobody,
My darling,
Could call me
A fussy man—

BUT

I do like a little bit of butter for my bread!"

THE STEADFAST TIN SOLDIER

by Hans Christian Andersen   translated by Carl Malmburg

Once upon a time there were twenty-five tin soldiers.

They were all brothers,

for they had been made from the same old tin spoon.

Each one stood stiffly at attention,

looking straight ahead and keeping his rifle shouldered.

with pictures by Michael Wood

And they all looked very smart
in their red and blue uniforms.
The very first thing they heard in this world,
when the lid was taken off their box,
was a little boy clapping his hands
and exclaiming, "Tin soldiers!"
They had been given to him as a birthday present,
and he immediately set them up on the table.

Each soldier looked exactly like the others,
except for one, who was just a little different.
He had only one leg,
for he had been poured into the mold last of all
and there had not been quite enough tin to finish him.
Nevertheless, he stood just as firmly on one leg
as the others did on their two,
and of all the soldiers he was the one
that people would some day hear about.

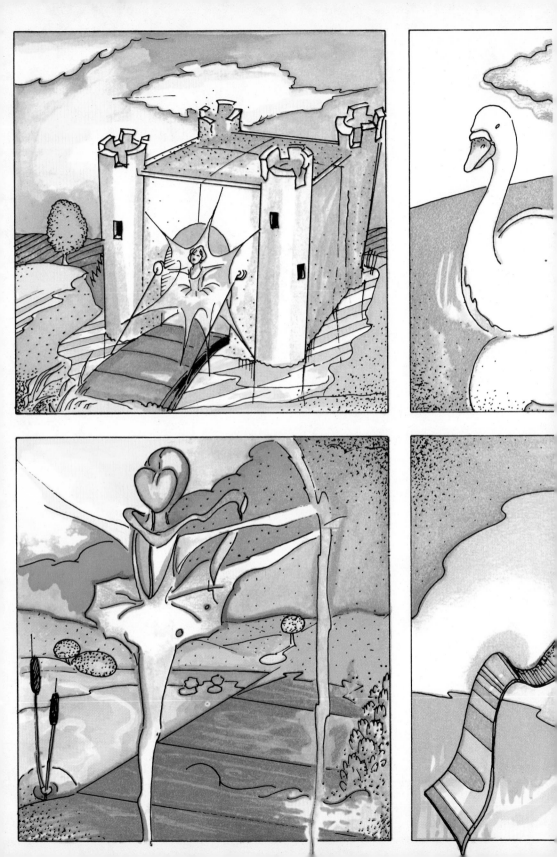

On the table there were many other toys,
but what caught the eye first
was a fine paper castle with tiny windows,
through which you could look and see the rooms inside.
Outside the castle, little trees had been placed
around a mirror which was a make-believe lake.
Wax swans floated on the surface of the mirror
and were reflected in it.
It was all very charming,
but prettiest of all was a little lady
who stood in the open doorway of the castle.
She too was cut out of paper,
but wore a skirt of sheerest linen,
and over her shoulder was draped a narrow blue ribbon
on which glittered a spangle as big as her face.
The little lady held both her arms outstretched,
for she was a dancer,
and she kicked one leg so high into the air
that the tin soldier could not see it.
So he thought that she, too,
had only one leg, as he did.
"Now, that's the very wife for me!" he thought.
"But she is a lady of high rank and lives in a castle,
whereas I have only a box,
and there are twenty-five of us sharing that.
No, that would be no place for her!
But anyway, I must try to make her acquaintance."

Then he stretched out behind a snuffbox that stood on the table. From there he could watch the charming little lady who stood on one leg without ever losing her balance. Late in the evening the other tin soldiers were put back into the box, and the people in the house went to bed. Then the toys began to play. They played paying visits, fighting battles, and giving parties. The tin soldiers rattled around in their box, for they wanted to join in the fun, but they could not lift the lid. The nutcracker turned somersaults, and the slate pencil scribbled on the slate. There was such a commotion that the canary woke up and began to join in the conversation—in verse, if you can believe such a thing! The only two who did not stir were the tin soldier and the little dancer. She remained poised on the tip of her toe with both her arms outstretched. He stood steadfastly on his one leg and did not for a moment take his eyes off her.

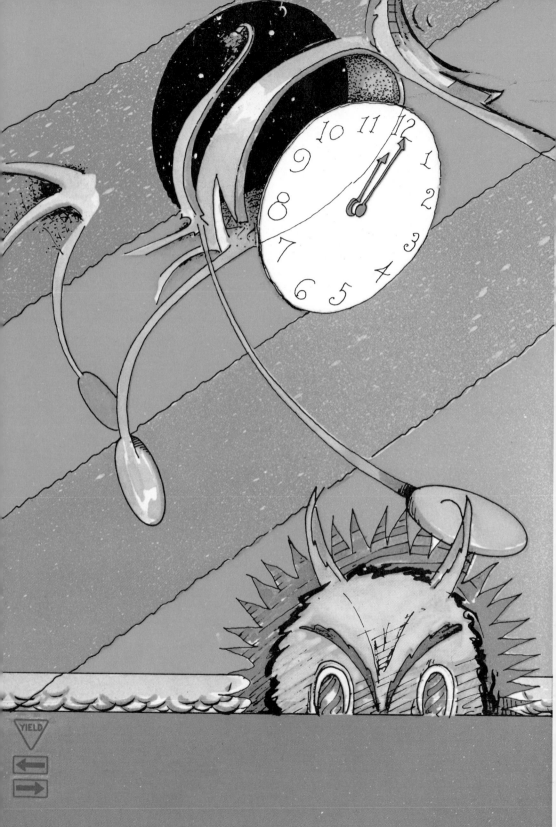

Then the clock struck midnight and — pop! — up snapped the lid of the snuffbox! But there was no snuff in it — instead, there was a little goblin. It was a trick snuffbox, you see, meant to startle people. "Tin soldier," said the goblin, "you had better keep your eyes to yourself!" But the tin soldier pretended not to hear. "All right!" said the goblin. "You just wait until tomorrow!"

The next morning, after the children got up, the tin soldier was moved over to the window sill. Whether what happened next was the work of the goblin or a gust of wind, we do not know, but suddenly the window flew open, and the soldier fell headlong from the third story. It was a terrifying fall. He landed with his head down, his one leg up in the air, and his bayonet stuck between two paving stones. The housemaid and the little boy ran down at once to look for him,

but although they almost stepped
on him, they did not see him. If the
tin soldier had cried out, "Here I
am!" they would surely have found
him, but he did not think it was
proper to shout when he was in uniform. Soon it began to rain. The
raindrops fell faster and faster, until it was a regular downpour. When
the storm was over, two street ur-
chins came along. "Look!" one of
them said,

"There's a tin soldier!

Let's send him for a sail."

So they made a boat out of an old newspaper, and put the tin soldier inside. Away he sailed down the gutter, while the boys ran along beside him clapping their hands. Goodness, what great waves there were in the gutter, and what a swift current! The paper boat pitched and tossed and whirled so fast that the tin soldier became quite dizzy. But he did not flinch or show the least sign of fear. He looked straight ahead and kept a firm hold on his rifle.

All of a sudden the boat was swept into a long drain pipe. There it was as dark as it had been in the box. "I wonder where I'm headed," the tin soldier thought. "If only I had the little lady here in the boat with me, it might be twice as dark and I shouldn't mind a bit!"

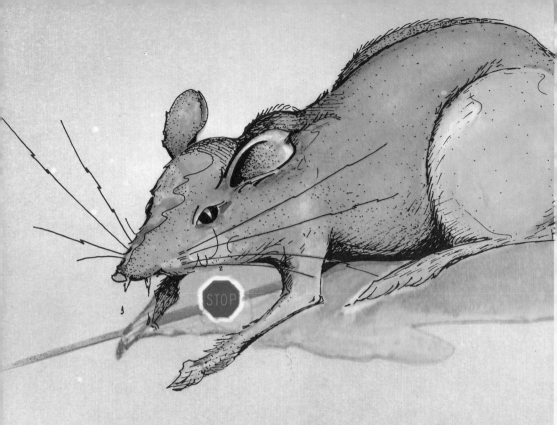

Just at that moment there appeared a huge water rat
who lived in the pipe.
"Have you a passport?" asked the rat. "Hand it over!"
The tin soldier did not answer,
but clasped his rifle tighter than ever.
The boat rushed on with the rat close behind it.
Oh, how he gnashed his teeth
and shouted to the sticks and straws
floating in the stream: "Stop him! Stop him! He didn't pay his toll!
He wouldn't show his passport!"
The current grew swifter and swifter.
Now the tin soldier could see daylight ahead,
but he heard a roaring noise

that was enough to frighten even the bravest of men.
Just think! Where the pipe ended,
the water emptied into a big canal.
The tin soldier felt as frightened
as you and I would if we were about
to be swept over a huge waterfall.
But now he was so close to the edge
that he could not escape.
The boat shot out into the canal,
while the tin soldier held himself as straight as he could—
nobody could say of him that he had
so much as blinked an eye.
The boat spun around three or four times
and filled with water to the brim.
It was sure to sink.
The tin soldier soon stood in water up to his neck,
and the boat sank deeper and deeper.
Now the paper began to come apart.
The soldier felt the water swirling about his head,
and as he went under he thought
of the lovely little dancer whom he would never see again.
In his ears rang the words of an old song:
"ONWARD! DANGER CALLS YOU, SOLDIER!
DEATH AWAITS YOU IN THE FIELD!"

Now the paper
boat gave way entire-
ly, and the tin soldier
plunged through the bottom.
Just then a big fish came along
and swallowed him. My, how dark
it was in the fish! It was even darker
than it had been in the pipe! And how
dreadfully cramped! But the tin soldier
remained as steadfast as ever, lying at
full length with his rifle still
shouldered.
The fish thrashed about in
a most frightful manner.
Then,
finally
it became

very quiet. After some
time, a flash of lightening
seemed to penetrate the
darkness. Suddenly it was
daylight again, and someone
exclaimed, "A tin soldier!" The fish had
been caught, taken to the market and
sold, and was now in the kitchen where
the maid had just cut it open with a big
knife. She picked the tin soldier up by
the waist, and with two fingers
carried him into the living room.
Everyone was eager to get a look
at such a remarkable fellow—
a tin soldier who had
traveled around in the
belly of a fish!

But the tin soldier did not let their admiration
go to his head.
They set him up on the table, and then
—what strange things do happen in this world!—
he found he was in the very same room
that he had been in before.
He saw the very same children.
The very same toys stood on the table—
there was the splendid castle,
and the lovely little dancer.
She was still standing poised on one leg
with the other high in the air.
Yes, she was steadfast, too.
The tin soldier was so deeply moved
that he almost shed tin tears,
but that of course was something
a soldier could never do.
So he gazed at her and she gazed at him,
but neither of them said a word.

At that moment, for no reason at all,
the little boy picked up the tin soldier
and threw him into the fireplace.
Without doubt,
it was the goblin in the snuffbox
who was to blame for it.
The tin soldier stood there lit up by the flames.
He began to feel terribly hot,
but whether the heat came from the fire,
or from the love burning within him,
he did not know.
The bright colors were gone from his uniform;
whether because of all he had been through
or because of grief, who can tell?
He gazed at the little lady and she gazed at him.
He felt himself melting away,
but he remained steadfast,
standing at attention,
shouldering his rifle.

Suddenly a door was opened.
A gust of wind caught the little dancer,
and, like a sylph, she fluttered into the fire
and landed right next to the tin soldier.
She burst into flame and was gone!
The tin soldier melted down to a lump,
and the next day,
when the housemaid emptied the ashes,
she found him in the shape of a little tin heart.
But all that was left of the dancer
was her spangle,
and that was burnt black as coal.

A Parade

A parade!   A parade!
A-rum-a-tee-tum
I know a parade
By the sound of the drum.
>A-rum-a-tee-tum
>A-rum-a-tee-tum
>A-rum-a-tee-tum-
>a-tee-tum.

Here it comes.
Down the street.
I know a parade
By the sound of the feet.

Music and feet
Music and feet
Can't you feel
The sound and the beat?
>A-rum-a-tee-tum
>A-rum-a-tee-tum
>A-rum-a-tee-tum-
>a-tee-tum.

by Mary Catherine Rose

The Picnic

We brought a rug for sitting on,
Our lunch was in a box.
The sand was warm. We didn't wear
Hats or Shoes or Socks.

Waves came curling up the beach.
We waded. It was fun.
Our sandwiches were different kinds.
I   my jelly one.
dropped

by Dorothy Aldis

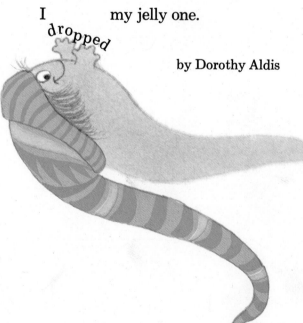

picture by George Buckett

Noodles
and the
MAIL BOX

A CONVERSATION THAT COULD BE ACTED OUT

(MUSIC DOWN-START SCENE)

Bill: Noodles! What are you doing in my mailbox?

Noodles: Oh, I'm just resting in here. Hello! Hello there, Bill Martin.

Bill: Any mail in there for me today?

Noodles: Yes, but it wasn't very interesting. Just three Christmas cards.

Bill: You've been reading my mail.

Noodles: I didn't get any, so I read yours.

Bill: Well, maybe you didn't write any letters. You know, you don't get letters if you don't write any.

Noodles: Well, come to think of it, I just forgot to mail my Christmas cards this year.

Bill: You did? Well, no wonder you didn't get any.

Noodles: Do you think it's too late to send them now?

Bill: Well, yes. It's Christmas Eve.

Noodles: Oh, well. Say, I'll sing my Christmas greetings right now. Suppose that'll be all right?

Bill: Well, I-I'm sure all your friends are listening. They would like to hear you.

Noodles: Oh, but-- only, I can't sing.

Bill: Of course you can. Everyone can sing.

Noodles: Oh-ho, you don't know. Well, sound your "do." Do-do. Re-re. Mi-mi. Hey, would you help me?

(He pulls Bill near to whisper in his ear.)

131

Bill: Well, if I could. O-oh! Don't bite me!

Noodles: Ehh--Come here, come here.

Bill: What?

Noodles: Well, don't sing too loud, will you?

Bill: No, I won't sing too loud. Boys and girls, Noodles wants to sing you his Christmas greetings, which he forgot to mail.

(MUSIC)

Noodles
and
Bill:

We wish you a Merry Christmas,
We wish you a Merry Christmas,
We wish you a Merry Christmas,
And a Happy New Year.

Oh, bring us some figgy pudding,
Oh, bring us some figgy pudding,
Oh, bring us some figgy pudding,
And bring some out here.

We won't go until we get some,
  We won't go until we get some,
We won't go until we get some,
  So bring some out here.

We wish you a Merry Christmas,
  We wish you a Merry Christmas,
We wish you a Merry Christmas,
  And a Happy New Year.

Noodles: *A very, very, very Happy New Year!*

(END OF SONG)

Noodles: Oh, beautiful, beautiful. Only you sang too loud.

Bill: Oh, Noodles.

Noodles: Well, I have such a lovely voice, don't I?

Bill: Yes, Noodles, you do.

Noodles: I'm going now and start addressing my Christmas cards for next year.

Noodles: Good-bye, Bill. Oodely, oodely!

Bill: Good-bye, Noodles. Oh, just a moment. Can you come over to the Wish Shop for a story? I'm going to tell a story in a moment.

Noodles: No, no, I'm too busy. But, uh, I'm wondering, would you, would you tell it about the night before Christmas?

Bill: Ooh, yes, I'd like to.

Noodles: You know that's my favorite story. "The Night Before Christmas." You won't forget to tell it now, will you?

Bill: Oh, no, no, I promise.

Noodles: Okay. Well, well, good-bye, good-bye. Oodely, oodely.

Bill: Good-bye, Noodles. Good-bye. We'll see you Christmas Day.

(MUSIC - THE END)

A Picture for Pondering
by Rasmussen

The Kind of Bath for Me

You can take a tub with a rub and a scrub
    in a two-foot tank of tin,
You can stand and look at the whirling brook
    and think about jumping in;
You can chatter and shake in the cold black lake,
    but the kind of bath for me,
Is to take a dip from the side of a ship,
    in the trough of the rolling sea.

You may lie and dream in the bed of a stream
    when an August day is dawning,
Or believe 'tis nice to break the ice
    on your tub of a winter morning;
You may sit and shiver beside the river,
    but the kind of bath for me,
Is to take a dip from the side of a ship,
    in the trough of the rolling sea.

by Sir Edward Parry,
picture by Eric Carle

The Park

I'm glad that I   For in the winter
Live near a park   After dark

The park lights shine
As bright and still

As dandelions
On a hill.

by James S. Tippett, picture by Gilbert Riswold

139

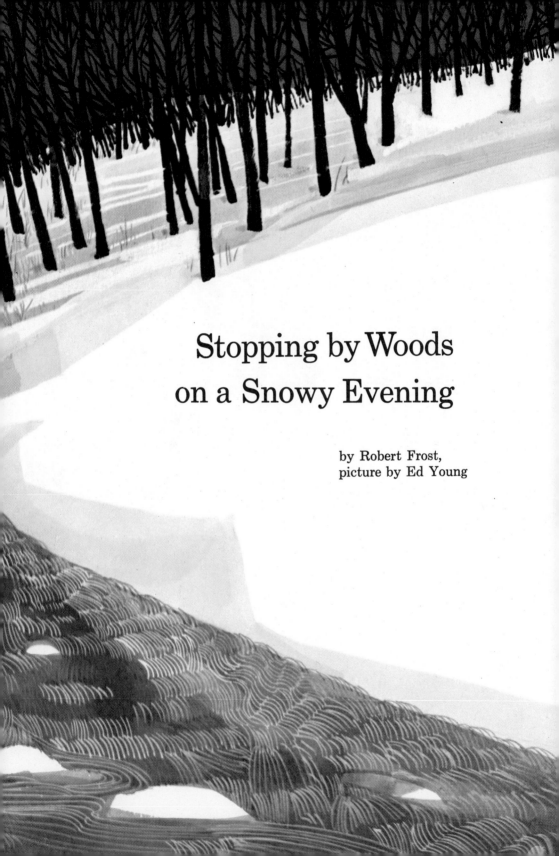

Stopping by Woods on a Snowy Evening

by Robert Frost,
picture by Ed Young

Whose woods these are I think I know.
His house is in the village though;
He will not see me stopping here
To watch his woods fill up with snow.

My little horse must think it queer
To stop without a farmhouse near
Between the woods and frozen lake
The darkest evening of the year.

He gives his harness bells a shake
To ask if there is some mistake.
The only other sound's the sweep
Of easy wind and downy flake.

The woods are lovely, dark, and deep.
But I have promises to keep,
And miles to go before I sleep,
And miles to go before I sleep.

Tomorrow

when the wind is high
I'll build a kite to ride the sky,
Tomorrow, when the wind is high.

Tomorrow when the waters gleam
I'll build a boat to sail the stream,
Tomorrow, when the waters gleam.

Tomorrow when the roads run far
Across the hills, I'll build a car.
I'll build a car with shining wheels
To pass the other automobiles,
Tomorrow, when the roads run far.

a poem by Rowena Bastin Bennett,
picture by Symeon Shimin

Can the Matter Be?

Something is the matter with Roger.
He thinks he is handsome.
There must be something the matter
with Roger to think he is
handsome.

Nothing is the matter with Harry
He knows he is not handsome.
To be sure he is unhandsome,
he breaths fire.

Oh dear! What!

story by Bill Martin Jr., pictures by Risa Glickman, lettering by Ray Barber

Everything is the
matter with Peter.
He knows everything
is the matter
so he acts like a
hippie.

Only one thing is
the matter
with Myrtle.
She is pretty.
She'd rather be
pretty than
be a dragon.
Her mother
can't change
her mind.

Not a thing is the matter with Joseph.
He looks like a crocodile
but when you're a dragon,
it doesn't matter if you look
like a crocodile.

Look what is the matter with Steven.
His tongue is stuck.
It is stuck outside.

Josephine also is stuck. She is stuck in her
stocking. Being stuck in a stocking
is a serious dragon matter.

Horace also has   a serious matter. He has
three heads. "But this is good," says Horace.
"Three heads are better than one in working
out a problem."

Sylvester is lucky.
He has found
a way
to solve his problem.

Mary is not lucky.
Her problem is
running away
with her.
Some problems
are like that.

Here's a Picture for Storytelling

by George Buckett

The Big Cheese

by Miriam Schlein,
pictures by Joseph Low

Once there was a farmer who made a big cheese.
It was yellow, and mellow, and round.
It was a most beautiful cheese.

"Without a doubt," said the farmer,
"this is the best cheese
that has ever been made in all the land."

"I think you are right," said his wife, taking a sniff.
"Take it to the market. It will fetch a good price."

"No," said the farmer.
"The best cheese in all the land—who should eat it?
Not just anybody! No," he said proudly.
"I am going to present this cheese to the king."

"The king!" said his wife. "To the king?"

"Of course," said the farmer.
"And even the king, when he has tasted,
will agree that this is the finest cheese
he has ever had in his life!"

He placed the big cheese carefully in a wheelbarrow.
His wife draped it over with a snowy white linen napkin.
And the farmer went down the road,
pushing the cheese before him.

He did not go too far, when he met a goatherd,
herding along a flock of goats.

"What are you pushing along in that barrow,
my friend?"
called out the goatherd.

"A cheese," replied the farmer,
setting down the wheelbarrow gently.
"I am on my way to present it to the king,
for it is the finest cheese
that has ever been made in the land."

"Indeed?" said the goatherd.
And is it made of goats' milk?"

"No," said the farmer. "Cows' milk."

"Then how," replied the goatherd,
"can it be the best cheese ever made?
The finest and richest and best cheeses
are always made from goats' milk."

"How?" said the farmer indignantly. "This is how!"
He flung the napkin off. And there sat the cheese—
that beautiful, yellow, mellow cheese.

"It does look fine," agreed the goatherd.
"But have you tasted it?"

"Of course not," said the farmer.
"You can see it is still whole."

"Then how do you *know*
it is the finest cheese ever made?

We must taste it, here and now,"
said the goatherd, pulling out a knife.

"Stop!" cried the farmer.
"How can I present the king with a cheese
that has a piece cut out of it?"

"But how can you
present the king with a cheese
you do not know tastes the best?"

"You are right," said the farmer. "Cut."

The goatherd cut out a large triangular slab.
This he cut in two,
half for the farmer, half for himself.

They each took a small taste.

"Indeed," sighed the goatherd.
"It is a fine-tasting cheese."

They sat in the shade, under a tree, nibbling cheese.
The goats nibbled the grass in a circle, all around them.

When they were finished, the farmer sprang up.
"I must be on my way," he said.

"I, too," said the goatherd. "Go well, my friend.
I must admit you have made the finest cheese
a man could make,
out of goats' milk, or cows' milk."

The farmer beamed.
He threw the napkin over the cheese and went on his way.
He followed the road over hill and dale.
As night began to fall, he came to an inn.

"I will stop here," he thought.
"I will have a bite to eat and get a good night's rest,
and early in the morning, I shall be on my way."

He pushed open the door,
which entered into a cheerful room,
all set with tables and cloths.
To one side, a big fire crackled in the fireplace.
Before the fire sat a fat, rather jolly-looking man.

"Come in," cried the fat man.
"The innkeeper is in the kitchen, fixing my meal.
But come warm yourself by the fire, my friend.
I am a traveler like yourself."

The farmer parked the barrow with the cheese
carefully away from the heat of the fire.

"And what have you there,
that you treat with such care?"
asked the man, curiously.

"I treat it with care indeed," replied the farmer.
"For this is a cheese, which I am taking to the king."

"To the king?" said the traveler.
"But the king has the most skilled cheese-makers
right at the palace!"

"But my cheese is the best
that has ever been made in the land," said the farmer.

"The best?" repeated the traveler. "How do you know?"

"I know," said the farmer, proudly.
"Besides, the goatherd agreed with me."

"The goatherd!" said the traveler.
"The goatherd may know about goats—
but what does he know of the king's taste for cheese?"

"I tell you what," he went on. "Sit down. Relax.
Do me the honor of dining with me.
After we have wined and dined,
and our stomachs are contented,
then *we*," he said, pointing to himself,
"then *we* will taste your cheese.
For it does not do to taste cheese when one is very hungry.
For then almost anything will taste delicious.
No, the time to taste cheese for delicacy of flavor
is when the stomach is already contented.
That is the way to taste cheese.
Ask me, my friend. I know!"

"But I want to present my cheese to the king!"
cried the farmer.

"Of course," said the traveler. "Don't fear.
We will just take a teeny taste. It won't even be missed.
Come now," he beckoned. "Here is the dinner.
Sit down with me, and enjoy it."

The farmer sighed, and sat down.

Presently the innkeeper came
and set before them all sorts of steaming hot dishes.
One was a platter of roast duck,
all crispy and brown on the outside.
There was stuffing, and brown gravy with mushrooms.
There were buttery beans and carrots,
and a tray of fresh-baked bread.
And to drink, there was a pitcher
of foamy homemade root beer.

"Ah," sighed the farmer, when they were finished.
"That was a meal to remember."

"And now," said the jolly traveler
sitting up in his chair, so that his big round body
seemed to fill every inch of it.
"Now we come to the treat of the meal.
Now we taste the cheese."

"The cheese," said the farmer.
"Are you sure you want to taste it now?
Aren't you a bit full?"

"Of course I'm full, of course," cried the jolly traveler.
"But if your cheese is as truly delicious as you say—
we will enjoy it even if we are full as full as full.
Bring it on!"
He whisked the napkin off the cheese.
"It *looks* good," he said.
Then he cut the cheese and took a small wedge.

He bit into the soft center,
and crushed the cheese on his tongue,
and swallowed.

"But the taste," he cried, striking the table.
"The taste is magnificent!
I have never tasted as good a cheese—
not even one made by myself!"

He wiped his hands of the crumbs.

"I must take another small piece."

"Mmmm," said the fat traveler,
with his mouth full.
"Mmmm. My friend," he said. "You are right.
This is a cheese fit for the king.
I'll take just one more taste."

"This is the last," promised the jolly traveler,
carving a large slice. "But here," he said.
"Don't you want a piece for yourself?
You haven't had any at all!"

"Oh, I'm too full," said the farmer unhappily,
as he watched his big cheese get smaller and smaller.

"There," said the fat traveling man, wiping his lips.
"Take it away."

The farmer leaped up, threw the napkin over the cheese,
and trundled it away. Then he said goodnight
and went up to his room to sleep.

In the morning early, the farmer awoke
and had a hearty breakfast.

Then he took his wheelbarrow, with the cheese,
and trundled it down the road.
It was a lovely day, sunny and bright.

The road led straight along.

The farmer walked briskly,
past field upon field of tall golden corn,
with tassels bending in the breeze.

And soon, in the distance,
he saw tall spires,
reaching into the sky.
"The king's palace,"
he said.
"I am there at last."

He straightened his shirt, pulled up his socks,
and presented himself at the palace gate.

"Who are you, and what do you carry?"
asked the guard at the gate.

"I am a farmer," said the farmer.
"And this is a cheese I have made for the king."

"That door," said the guard.
He pointed across the courtyard,
to where three young fellows were stringing beans,
and a woman was beating a batter.

"There is the royal kitchen."

"But this cheese is to be presented to the king himself!" said the farmer, determinedly.

"Then that other door," said the guard. He pointed to a high, arched doorway.

The farmer trundled across the courtyard and through the high arched door. He found himself alone in a large hall.

But from behind a closed doorway
at the other end of the hall, he heard a hum of voices.

Presently the door opened and a man came out.
He was dressed in elegant ribbons and silk,
with a plumed hat on his head.

When he saw the farmer and his barrow,
he said, surprised, "Eh, what is that?"

"A big cheese," said the farmer.
"I wish to present it to the king."

"A cheese, you say?" said the man with interest.
"Ah, a bit of cheese would taste good."

"Besides," he added, "I am the king's taster.
Whatever the king eats, I must taste first.
To make sure it is all right, you understand.
I had best do it now."

He bent down and with his silver penknife
cut off a wedge of the cheese.

"Indeed," he said, with his mouth full.
"It is a fine cheese."

"Now, may I present it to the king?" asked the farmer.

The taster's mouth was too full to answer.
Just then, the door opened again
and another man came out.
He was even more elegantly dressed than the first,
in varying shades of deep maroon,
with tassels and braids of gold.

"What are you doing?" he asked in amazement,
seeing the farmer with the barrow,
and the first man with his silver penknife in hand.

"Cheese," the first man managed to say. "Very good."

"Ah," said the second man,

unclasping a little gold penknife, and making a cut

Another, then another of the king's men came out.

Soon there were seven, all standing about,

with their delicate little knives in hand,

all munching on the cheese.

Presently still another man came out
from the room at the end of the hall,
closing the door behind him.

He was of medium height, the same as the farmer.
He had a ruddy face, as if he spent
much of his time out of doors.

And he was not dressed as splendidly
as the other men of the court.
but the other men stepped back
when he approached. "What is this?" he said.

"A cheese, sir," said the farmer, stepping forward.
"The best that has ever been made in all the land.
And who should eat the best cheese?
Not just anybody. No.
It is a cheese fit for a king.
And that is why I am here.
I have come to present it to the king!"

"Indeed?" said the ruddy-faced man, lifting the napkin.
The farmer stared. For what was left of his big cheese?
Not a half. Not even a quarter.
Just a small piece stood there, amidst the crumbles.

The ruddy-faced man bent down,
and reached for the last piece.

"Stop!" cried the farmer.
His voice rang out in the large hall.
"Stop, stop, STOP!"

The others looked up in amazement.

"Excuse me," said the farmer, sadly.
"But I meant this cheese for the king.
And you are taking the very last piece.
Well, take it," he said, turning sadly.

"It doesn't matter now.

I traveled all this way,

but I can't present the king with just a scrap.

Go on," he said. "Finish it."

   "But I am the king," the ruddy-faced man said, softly.

   "The king!" said the farmer. "A thousand pardons!"

   He bent his head, and fell to one knee,

nearly tipping the barrow as he did so.

   "Come," said the king. "Get up.

A thousand pardons? A thousand pardons for what?

For your loyalty to the king?

For wishing to present to him the finest cheese

you have ever made in your life?

"Come now," he said.
"There is nothing to pardon. Get up."

The farmer got up, all red in the face.

"May I have this last piece of cheese now?"
asked the king with a smile.
"I do love cheese, you know."

"Of course," the farmer nodded.

The king ate the piece of cheese.
"It is the finest cheese I have ever tasted
in all my life!" he said.
"And I thank you."

The farmer beamed. "But such a small piece was left,"
he said. "I am sorry."

"Look here," said the king.
"This is not the last cheese
you will ever make in your life, is it?"

"No." The farmer shook his head.

"Well then," said the king,
"when you make another cheese
which you feel you would like me to have,
just bring it around.
And do not let anyone taste it first," he added.
"I will trust your very own judgment."

To this the farmer agreed.
Then he trundled his empty wheelbarrow back home,
whistling all the way.

How glad he was to be home!
He told his wife his adventures.
Then he busied himself on his farm
with his chickens, and his soft brown cows,
and his asparagus and pumpkin garden.
And of course, he made cheeses.

They were fine cheeses, yellow
and mellow and round.
But somehow, none seemed yellow
and mellow enough so as to be fit for a king.

Many months passed. Almost a year.
Then one day, the farmer ran in, to his wife.

"I have made one!" he cried. "At last!"

"Fit for a king?" asked his wife.

"Fit for a king!"

With not another word,
they placed the big cheese on the wheelbarrow.
The farmer's wife covered it
with a gleaming white linen napkin.

And the farmer set off, down the road,
to the palace of the king.

Not the goatherd,
nor the jolly traveler,
nor the king's own men,
nor anyone else took a taste of *this* cheese.

This cheese the farmer presented to the king
round, and complete, and unbroken.

It was every bit as good as the first one.
It was a cheese fit for a king!

That is what the king said.
And he should know!

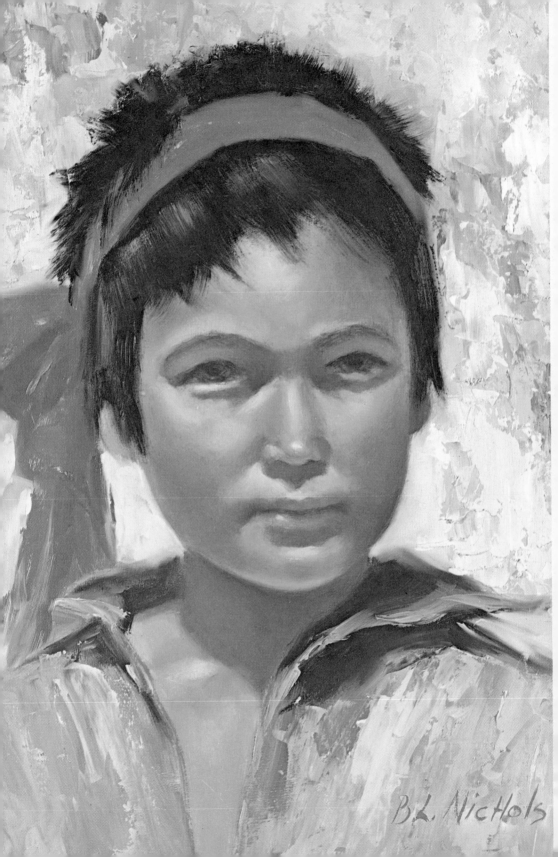

B.L. Nichols

excerpted from translations by George W. Cronyn, painting by B. L. Nichols

Songs of the Navajo

In beauty may I walk.
All day long may I walk.
Through the returning seasons may I walk.
On the trail marked with pollen may I walk.
With grasshoppers about my feet may I walk.
With dew about my feet may I walk.
With beauty may I walk.
With beauty before me, may I walk.
With beauty behind me, may I walk.
With beauty above me, may I walk.
With beauty below me, may I walk.
With beauty all around me, may I walk.
In young age wandering on a trail of beauty,
    lively, may I walk.
In old age wandering on a trail of beauty,
    lively, may I walk.
It is begun in beauty.
It is begun in beauty.

The curtain of darkness is hanging,
From the land of night it is hanging,
Before me, in beauty, it is hanging,
Behind me, in beauty, it is hanging,
Above me, in beauty, it is hanging,
Below me, in beauty, it is hanging.
How joyous the darkness!
Hanging before me,
    behind me,
        above me,
            below me,
How joyous, how joyous the stars!

painting by Richard W. Davidson

The curtain of daybreak is hanging,
The daylight curtain is hanging,
From the land of day it is hanging,
Before me, as it dawns, it is hanging,
Behind me, as it dawns, it is hanging,
Above me, in daylight, it is hanging,
Below me, in daylight, it is hanging,
How joyous the daylight!
Hanging before me,
    behind me,
        above me,
            below me,
In beauty,
In beauty it is hanging!

Beauty before me,
    With it I wander.
Beauty behind me,
    With it I wander.
Beauty below me,
    With it I wander.
Beauty above me,
    With it I wander.
In young age traveling,
    With it I wander.
In old age traveling,
    With it I wander.
On the beautiful trail I am,
    With it I wander.

painting by F. Koufmann

Thonah! Thonah!
  There is a voice above
    Sounding in the dark cloud,
      The voice of the thunder
        Thonah! Thonah!
        Thonah! Thonah!
          There is a voice below,
            The voice of the grasshopper.
            The earth is rumbling
              From the beating of our basket drums.
              The cloud is rumbling
                From the beating of our basket drums.
                Everywhere humming,
                Everywhere rumbling,
                Everywhere raining,
                Raining,
                Raining.

painting by Maynard Dixon

That flowing water!
That flowing water!
My mind wanders across it.
That broad water!
That flowing water!
My mind wanders across it.
That old age water!
That flowing water!
My mind wanders across it.

watercolor by Allen Reinhold, painting (next page) by Cornelius Salisbury

In beauty have I walked.
All day long have I walked.
All life long have I walked.
Through the returning seasons have I walked.
On the trail marked with pollen have I walked.
With grasshoppers about my feet have I walked.
With dew about my feet have I walked.
With beauty have I walked.
With beauty before me, have I walked.
With beauty behind me, have I walked.
With beauty above me, have I walked.
With beauty below me, have I walked.
With beauty all around me, have I walked.
In young age wandering on a trail of beauty,
    lively, have I walked.
In old age wandering on a trail of beauty,
    lively, have I walked.
In old age wandering on a trail of beauty,
    living again, may I walk.
It is finished in beauty.
It is finished in beauty.

drawing by an unknown artist

COUNTING
LIGHTLY

by Leonard Simon,
pictures by Ted Schroeder

Father: "Come on, Dim. It's time to go.

Today you will learn to be a hunter."

Dim: "Today is the day," thought Dim.

"I will be a great hunter like my father.

I'm coming, Father! I'm ready!"

Father: "And what are you going to do with that spear, Dim?"

Dim: "I'm going to hunt buffalo."

Father: "Yes, but first you must learn to find them.

Do you see that tree?

Go hide under it.

If you see any buffalo, come back and tell me."

Dim: "Whew! It's hot up here!" thought Dim.

"Hunting is hard work.

I haven't seen a buffalo all day.

Gee, I'm tired.

Maybe I can take a little nap."

Dim jumped up.

Dim: "What was that?

What makes the earth shake so?

I see them now.

There are the buffalo.

There are so many of them.

There are more than a dog has legs!

There are more than I have friends!

I must tell everybody!"

A stage direction:

Dim ran down the hill.

Dim: "I found them!

I found the buffalo!" he shouted.

Father: "How many, Dim? How many did you see?"

Dim: "I saw more than a tree has branches,

more than there are stars in the sky."

Sister: "Oh Dim, you did not," said his sister.

"You're just making it up."

Dim: "I am not!" said Dim.

"I saw a whole bunch."

Sister: "How many?"

Dim: "I don't know."

Father: "Dim," said his father, "a great hunter must know

how many animals he sees."

Dim: "All right. I'll go back and look,

and then I'll tell you how many."

Dim: "But how can I count all the buffalo?" thought Dim.

"I wish I could carry each buffalo back.

That way I would not have to count them.

But they are too heavy.

I will never be able to be a hunter."

A stage direction: Dim lay down on the hillside.

Dim: "Lying on the rocks hurts my knees.

The rocks! That gives me an idea!

I know how I can count the buffalo."

Announcer: How do you think Dim will count the buffalo?

Dim: "I cannot carry buffalo.

But I can carry rocks.

One rock for one buffalo.

Another rock for another buffalo.

This is easy.

Now, all I have to do is carry the rocks

down the hill."

Dim: "These rocks are heavy," said Dim.

"I don't think I can carry them all.

It's hard to carry rocks

and slide down the hill at the same time.

Oops, dropped one.

Oops, there goes another!

I can't carry so many in my hands.

I saw more buffalo than I have rocks.

I dropped buffalos... I mean

A stage direction: I dropped rocks all the way down the hill."

Everybody laughed.

Father: "Dim, isn't there something lighter than rocks

that you could carry?"

Dim: Dim thought, "I always carry wood for the fire."

"I know," he said.

"I'll carry back a stick of wood for each buffalo.

There are many sticks up on the hill."

Dim: "This is easy," said Dim.

"One stick for one buffalo.

Two sticks for two buffalo.

Another stick for another buffalo."

A stage direction: Soon Dim had a pile of sticks —

one stick for each buffalo.

Dim: "This pile of sticks is hard to carry.

There, I came all the way down the hill

and didn't drop one.

Now, everybody can count my sticks.

The number of sticks is the same

as the number of buffalo."

Dim: "I saw as many buffalo as I have sticks," said Dim.

"Now you can see how many buffalo there are.

But my arms hurt from carrying the sticks.

I'm getting too tired to hunt.

I wish there were a lighter way to count."

Sister: "Dim," said his sister,

"you could count the buffalo with only one stick."

Dim: "I could not!" said Dim. "There are many buffalo."

Sister: "Come on," said his sister, "I'll show you.

Just bring that long stick and that rock."

Announcer: Can you guess how Dim's sister

will count the buffalo?

Sister: "Now Dim, you watch," said his sister.

"There is one buffalo.

I make one mark on the stick.

There is another buffalo.

I make another mark on the stick."

Dim: "Now I see," said Dim. "I can do the rest."

Dim brought his stick to his father.

Dim: "See how many buffalo there are!

And it isn't so hard to carry just one stick."

Sister: "Dim," said his sister, "you can count
without carrying anything."

Dim: "Count without carrying anything? How?"

Sister: "Use your fingers. Look, Dim!

One finger for one buffalo.

Two fingers for two buffalo.

Another finger for another buffalo."

Dim: "Is that so! But I don't *have* enough fingers

to tell how many buffalo I saw."

Sister: "It doesn't matter, Dim.

When you use up all your fingers,

you can start over again."

Dim: "That's silly."

Sister: "When you use up all your fingers,

just think *all*.

Here, I'll draw a picture to show you.

See, these are like the marks on the stick.

This many means *all*.

So, you saw *all*-and-two buffalo."

A stage direction:

Dim looked at his sister.

He looked at the picture of the stick.

Dim: "You never use rocks, or sticks, or fingers.
　　　How come you can count?"

Sister: "Oh, I use words," said his sister.
　　　"I made up names to count with.
　　　And using counting names is easy—
　　　all you have to do is remember them.
　　　You can think them, and say them,
　　　and write them, and read them.
　　　And they are never heavy to carry."

Dim: "And then," said Dim,
　　　"you really are counting lightly."

POOR LADY she swallowed a fly,

I don't know why she swallowed a fly.

Poor old lady, I think she'll die.

POOR LADY she swallowed a spider.

It squirmed and wriggled and turned inside her.

She swallowed the spider to catch the fly.

I don't know why she swallowed a fly.

Poor old lady, I think she'll die.

POOR LADY she swallowed a bird.

How absurd! She swallowed a bird.

She swallowed the bird to catch the spider,

She swallowed the spider to catch the fly,

I don't know why she swallowed a fly.

Poor old lady, I think she'll die.

POOR LADY she swallowed a cat.

Think of that! She swallowed a cat.

She swallowed the cat to catch the bird.

She swallowed the bird to catch the spider,

She swallowed the spider to catch the fly,

I don't know why she swallowed a fly.

Poor old lady, I think she'll die.

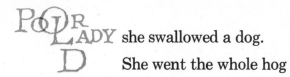

POOR LADY she swallowed a dog.
        She went the whole hog
                when she swallowed the dog.
    She swallowed the dog to catch the cat,
    She swallowed the cat to catch the bird,
    She swallowed the bird to catch the spider,
    She swallowed the spider to catch the fly.
    I don't know why she swallowed a fly.
    Poor old lady, I think she'll die.

POOR LADY she swallowed a cow.
        I don't know how
                she swallowed the cow.
    She swallowed the cow to catch the dog,
    She swallowed the dog to catch the cat,
    She swallowed the cat to catch the bird,
    She swallowed the bird to catch the spider,
    She swallowed the spider to catch the fly,
    I don't know why she swallowed a fly.
    Poor old lady, I think she'll die.

POOR LADY she swallowed a horse. She died, of course.

an old jingle

213

Paulossie

AN ESKIMO BOY

story and photographs of Eskimo stone carvings created by Robert C. Swim

This is Paulossie.
He lives in the North,
where the wind blows strong and cold.
But Paulossie is not cold.
He wears the sealskin parka
and the sealskin boots called *komiks*
that his mother made for him.

Paulossie's father, Tagoona, is a good hunter.
He has a pair of good binoculars
and a powerful rifle.
One day Paulossie borrowed his father's binoculars
and went up to the high rocky hill behind his igloo.
He wanted to watch the animals that lived on the ice.
Through the binoculars Paulossie watched
two walruses sleeping on the ice.

Suddenly he saw a great polar bear
swimming toward the two sleeping walruses.
The polar bear swam closer.
Then he climbed onto the ice and with his teeth
grabbed the nearest walrus by the nose and mouth
so that the walrus could not use its sharp tusks.

The walrus cried out, and fought the polar bear. But he was caught.

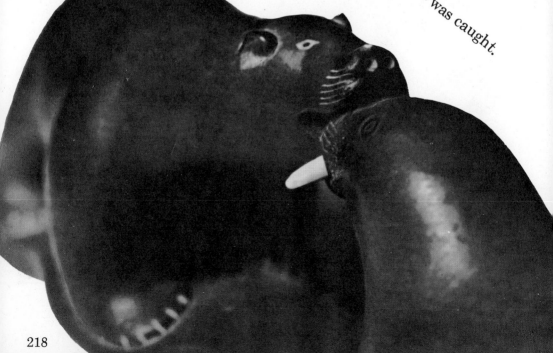

The other walrus woke up and slipped quickly into the water.
There was nothing he could do to help his friend.
It was too late. The polar bear was going to have his dinner.
"The poor walrus," thought Paulossie.

Paulossie picked up the binoculars
and looked down on the lake at the foot of the hill.
He saw a little duck, swimming alone.
Suddenly a snowy white owl swooped down from the sky.
The duck dived under the water, but too late.
The owl caught the duck by the back of the neck
and lifted him out of the water.
"The poor duck," thought Paulossie.
Paulossie stood up and started down the hill.
He felt very sorry about the walrus and about the duck.

At the bottom of the hill Paulossie saw Niki,
one of his father's dogs.
Niki was chewing on a piece of ice-covered fish.
Tagoona, Paulossie's father,
had caught the fish through a hole in the ice,
and it had frozen solid as soon as it was taken from the water.
The fish Niki ate were always frozen.
He had to work hard for every bite.
Paulossie said, "Hello, Niki."
But as Paulossie came closer, Niki growled.
Niki did not like to have anyone near him when he was eating.
He was afraid his food
would be taken away from him.

"It is a very hard world,"
Paulossie said.
"First I saw the polar bear
attack the walrus.
Then I saw
the snowy white owl
attack the little duck.
And now here is Niki,
growling
because he is afraid
I will take the fish."

When Paulossie arrived home,
his mother Mary, was sitting in front of the igloo.
She was working very hard.
She was chewing a piece of sealskin to make it soft.
She was getting this piece of sealskin ready
to make komiks for Paulossie's little brother, Davidie.
If Mary didn't chew the sealskin,
it would be too tough to make into komiks.
It would cut the threads
when she sewed it,
and the water
would seep through
and wet little
Davidie's
feet.

So Mary had to make the sealskin soft before she sewed it.

Mary looked up as Paulossie came near the igloo.

"You look sad, Paulossie," she said.

"What is the matter?"

"I think it is a very hard world, Mother,"
  said Paulossie.

"This morning I saw a polar bear attack a walrus
  that was sleeping on the ice.
  I saw a snowy white owl swoop down on a little duck.
  Then Niki growled at me when I came near him
  while he was eating a fish.
  Why is it that way?"

Mary slowly pushed back the hood of her parka.
  Quietly she began,

"Do you remember when you were a baby,
  how you cried when we had no food to give you?"

"No," said Paulossie.

"I was too little to remember."
  Mary said,

"Do you remember when you were a small boy,
  and your father could not catch any animals or fish?
  Do you remember how you cried
  from the pains in your stomach?"

"Yes," said Paulossie, "I remember that."

"Within all creatures," said Mary,

"there is a voice that cries, 'Live! Live! Live!'
  When we do not listen to that voice,
  it makes us hear it in another way.
  All creatures have pain when they are hungry,
  or when they are very tired,
  or when they are cold."

"If we do not have enough to eat,
our stomachs pinch and hurt us.
If we do not get enough sleep,
our eyes and our head hurt.
If we do not dress warmly enough,
we shiver
and shake,
and our teeth
begin
to chatter."

"Many times you have seen
your father standing
beside a hole in the ice,"
Mary said,
"out in the cold
for hours and hours.
He is waiting
for a seal
to come up for air.
When it does,
your father is able
to harpoon the seal,
pull it out of the water,
and quickly butcher it
right there on the ice
before it freezes solid.
If he waited,
he would not be able
to cut the seal
with his knife.
Then he sews up the seal
and brings it home
on a sled.
That is how we get
sealskins to make clothing,
and oil for our fire,
and food
for our hungry stomachs.
If your father
did not harpoon the seal,
we would not stay alive."

"When we are young, our parents
help us to stay alive.
When we grow older,
we must take care of ourselves.
One day soon, Paulossie,
you will go with your father
to harpoon the whale and the walrus,
for you, too, must learn how
to keep yourself alive.
That is also why
he traps the fox,
and goes out in his kayak
to harpoon the whale and the walrus.
We must have the skins
and the oil and the meat to live.
All creatures want to live,"
Mary continued.
"The polar bear attacks the walrus
because he wants to live.
The owl attacks the little duck
and hungry Niki guards his food
because they want to live.
And your father stands out in the cold,
near a hole in the ice,
waiting to harpoon a seal,
because he wants to live."

Just then Little Davidie
came out of the igloo.
He came out to see
if his komiks were finished.
But he was not dressed
for the cold air.
"Paulossie," said Mary,
"will you take Davidie
back inside the igloo, please,
until I finish his boots?
He is in a hurry for them."
"Yes, I will, Mother,"
said Paulossie.
Paulossie took Davidie
inside the igloo.
Mary finished
softening the sealskin
for little Davidie's komiks.
Paulossie played
with his little brother
while they waited for Tagoona
to come home
with something to eat.
Already
Paulossie's stomach
was telling him
it was time for supper.

The Snare

I hear a sudden cry of pain!
    There is a rabbit in a snare:
Now I hear the cry again,
    But I cannot tell from where.

But I cannot tell from where
    He is calling out for aid;
Crying on the frightened air,
    Making everything afraid,

Making everything afraid,
    Wrinkling up his little face,
As he cries again for aid;
    —And I cannot find the place!

And I cannot find the place
    Where his paw is in the snare;
Little one! Oh, little one!
    I am searching everywhere!

by James Stephens,
picture by Cynthia Koehler

tasty
wretched
disgusting
miserable
pesky

try as I might
since I wasn't there
so I can't tell
for the life of me

I don't know why she swallowed a

surely
certainly
really

PUZZLE

and saved her life.
and lived happily ever after.
and become famous.
to let in some air.
that flies are not for eating.

fly .

when she could have swallowed ice cream
when she could have chewed tobacco
when she could have played the piano
when she only opened her mouth
when her mother always told her

*How much longer can you make this sentence
by adding single words and clusters of words?*

WHEN SAMMY PUT THE PAPER ON THE WALL.

WHEN SAMMY STUCK TOGETHER A FEATHER WE ALL OF BIRDS LIKE

WHEN HE SPILLED THE POT OF THE PASTE UPON US ALL.

a traditional song, drawing and lettering by Bob Shein

WHEN SAMMY PUT THE PAPER ON THE WALL

Verse 1 When I was just a little girl (boy)
          I asked my mother, "What will I be?
          Will I be pretty (handsome)? Will I be rich?"
          Here's what she said to me:

Chorus   "Que sera, sera,
              Whatever will be will be;
              The future's not ours to see.
          Que sera, sera!
          What will be will be!"

Whatever Will Be, Will Be

Verse 2 When I was just a child in school,
          I asked my teacher, "What should I try?
          Should I paint pictures? Should I sing songs?"
          This was her wise reply:

Verse 3 When I grew up and fell in love,
          I asked my lover (sweetheart) "What lies ahead?
          Will we have rainbows day after day?"
          Here's what my lover (sweetheart) said:

Verse 4 When I have children of my own,
          They ask their mother (father) "What will I be?
          Will I be pretty (handsome)? Will I be rich?"
          I tell them tenderly:

a song by Jay Livingston and Ray Evans　　　　　picture by Zunia

a-sort-of-a-fairytale by Paulette Washington, age 10,
pictures by Tim and Greg Hildebrandt.

Tiger Boy

Way in the country
 in a little house
  lived a boy named Bill
but people called him
Tiger Boy
because he liked tigers.
 Every morning
   he would go looking for a tiger
    but instead of finding a tiger
    he found a cat
     and named it Tom.
      It was a gray and white cat.

Every morning he would feed the cat
except for one day
when he didn't have any food.
So Tom got angry
and began to bite Tiger Boy
and Tiger Boy got angry too,

and picked up Tom
and put him in a cage
and kept him in there.

Then he heard a knock at the door.
It was a big old lady
and before Tom asked her her name,
he said, Have a seat.
Then he said, My name is Bill,
and the old lady said,
My name is Mrs. Clark.
I was looking for a home
              until I came to this house.
                    Is this your cat?

Yes, said Tiger Boy,
his name is Tom.
I put him in the cage
because he was
hungry and
I didn't have
any food
to give him.

Oh! said the old lady. I have plenty food and plenty money for you and me.

Half the time they munched the grass,
   and all the time they lay
Down in the water-meadows,
   the lazy month of May,
     A-chewing,
     A-mooing,
To pass the hours away.   "Nice weather," said the brown cow.
                    "Ah," said the white.
            "Grass is very tasty."
                "Grass is all right."

Half the time they munched the grass,
   and all the time they lay
Down in the water-meadows,
   the lazy month of May,
     A-chewing,
     A-mooing,
To pass the hours away.   "Rain coming," said the brown cow.
                    "Ah," said the white.
           "Flies is very tiresome."
              "Flies bite."

Half the time they munched the grass,
   and all the time they lay
Down in the water-meadows,
   the lazy month of May,
     A-chewing,
     A-mooing,
To pass the hours away.

"Time to go," said the brown cow.
     "Ah," said the white.
  "Nice chat." "Very pleasant."
     "Night." "Night."

Half the time they munched the grass,
   and all the time they lay
Down in the water-meadows,
   the lazy month of May,
     A-chewing,
     A-mooing,
To pass the hours away.

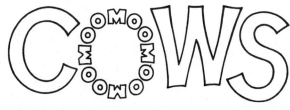

by James Reeves, picture by Mamoru Funai

I'm looking over a four leaf clover that I overlooked before;

One leaf is sunshine, the second is rain,

Third is the roses that grow in the lane,

No need explaining, the one remaining is somebody I adore. I'm looking over a four leaf clover that I overlooked before.

a song by Mort Dixon, illustration by Lynda Barber, handlettered by Ray Barber

The Story of TOM THUMB

Traditional, adapted by Bill Martin, Jr.
Pictures by Peter Lippman

*O*nce on a cold winter night long, long ago,
a woodcutter sat by the fire,
stirring the flames with a stick.
His wife sat near him,
at her spinning wheel, working.

"Oh, I wish we had a child," he said.
"All I hear is the sound of the wind
whistling at the door.
I would much rather hear
the sound of children playing on the floor."

"Yah, yah," said his wife. "If only we had a child,
even if he were no bigger than my thumb,
that would be having my heart's desire."

In due time, a child was born
to the woodcutter and his wife,
and though he was perfect in every way,
alas! he was no bigger than his mother's thumb.
He was so small that his mother could cradle him
in the palm of her hand.
"Oh, what a beautiful child he is,"
said the woodcutter's wife.

"Yah, yah," said the woodcutter.
"He's the handsomest child in the village."

Though they fed him plenty of rich nourishment,
he grew no larger and remained always
the size that he was first born,
no larger than his mother's thumb.
And they called him *Tom Thumb*.

One day many years later, when Tom's father
was going into the forest to cut wood,
he chanced to say, "Oh, if only I had someone
who could bring the horse and the cart
to me this afternoon,
it would make my work so much easier."

"I can bring the horse and cart to you, Father,"
said Tom.

"How could you do that, Tom?
You are so little,
you could not hold the reins in your hands."

"I don't need to hold the reins, Father.
If Mother will harness the horse to the cart
and put me in the horse's ear,
I'll simply tell the horse which way to go."

"Do you think it will work, Tom?
Very well, we'll try!"

So late that afternoon,
Tom's mother hitched the horse to the cart
and put Tom Thumb in the horse's ear.

Tom waved goodbye.

Then he shouted, "Gee up! Gee up!"

and the horse started down the road,

quite as if someone were sitting on the driver's seat,

tugging at the reins and telling him which way to go.

As the horse was turning a corner

and going into the woods

and Tom was shouting, "Gee up! Gee up!"

two strangers passed by.

The first stranger said, "This is very odd.

I see the horse, I hear the driver.

But alas! I cannot see him!"

"This is very odd, indeed!"
said the second stranger.
"Let's follow that horse and cart
and see to whom they belong."

The two strangers followed along until the horse
reached the spot where the woodcutter worked.
Tom Thumb called out, "Whoa! Here I am, Father,
with the horse and cart, just as I said.
Come take me from the horse's ear."

The woodcutter lifted the little boy
from the horse's ear
and held him in the palm of his hand.

The two strangers were surprised to see Tom Thumb.
They had never seen a child so small.

The first stranger said, "Let's buy that little boy
and show him on the street corners in town.
We'll make a fortune."

The second stranger said, "Didn't you hear?
He's a woodcutter's son.
The woodcutter will not sell his own son."

"Then let's take him," said the first stranger.
"There are two of us, but only one of him."

So the first stranger approached the woodcutter
and said, "Sell us that little boy, woodcutter.
We'll see that no harm comes to him."

"Oh, no, no!" said the woodcutter.
"I wouldn't sell my own son."

But Tom Thumb had overheard the evil men talking
and quickly climbed up to his father's shoulder
and whispered in his ear,
"You might as well take their gold, Father,
because they plan to carry me off, anyway.
But don't worry! I'll be home soon, very soon!"

And so it was that Tom Thumb was sold
for a double handful of gold,
and the tiny boy was carried away
by the two strangers.
He sat on the brim of the taller man's hat
and watched the countryside
as the strangers walked along the road.

At eventide, the two men were tired
from having walked so long and so far,
and they sat down at the crossroads to rest.
Tom Thumb was tired, too,
from having sat so long,
and he begged to be put down upon the road
to stretch his legs.

This was when the two strangers
made their mistake!
For when Tom Thumb was put down upon the road,
he darted off into a cornfield
where he found a mousehole just his size.
And he slipped down into it.

Just before he disappeared from sight,
he called out, "Goodbye, you evil men!
Your gold has fallen into a mousehole!
You'll never find me!"

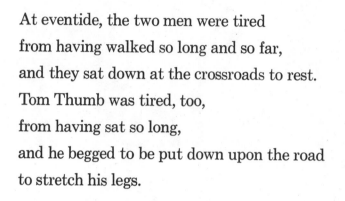

The two men were angry.
They ran up and down the rows of corn,
punching sticks into every mousehole,
but alas! they could not find Tom Thumb.

At last it became dark
and the two men had to hurry on their way,
because they knew their wives
were waiting supper on them.

When Tom Thumb was certain
that the two strangers had left,
he crawled out of the mousehole.
He didn't want to chance meeting
a big ferocious animal, like a mouse,
in its hole after dark.
So he walked along a row of corn
until he found a snail shell just his size.
He curled up in it and fell asleep.

But no sooner was Tom Thumb asleep,
when he was awakened by two robbers talking.

The first robber said,
"Let's go to the rich man's house
  and steal his gold and silver."

The second robber said,
"How can we get into his house?
  There are heavy iron bars at the window."

Tom Thumb called out, "I can help you!"

"Who said that?" asked the first robber.

"I did," said Tom Thumb.

"I am right at the toe of your boot.
  Don't move your foot,
  you might step on me.
  Just follow the sound of my voice
  and you'll find me."

The first robber grabbed Tom Thumb
  and held him tight in his fist.
"You little imp! How can you help us?"

"Oh, I can help you," said Tom.
"You want someone to walk through
  the iron bars of the rich man's house
  and hand out his gold and silver?
  I am the very person who can do that."

The robber smiled.
"Young man, you have quite a wit about you.
  We can use you!"

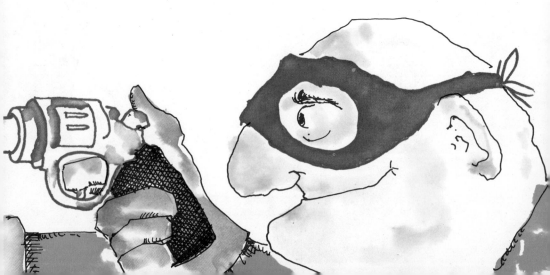

The robbers sneaked to the rich man's house
and put Tom Thumb on the window sill.
He was so small that he simply walked between
the iron bars and made his way into the house.

As soon as he was out of reach
of the robber's long arms,
he called out loudly,

What do you want first, the gold or the silver?

"Shhhhhh!" whispered the robbers.
"Do you want to awaken everyone in the house,
  you little fool?"

The housemaid awakened.
She lit a candle and came down the stairs,
looking fearfully about.
"What's going on down here?" she asked.

On hearing someone coming,
the robbers turned and fled into the forest.
They were never heard from again.

The housemaid looked all about,
behind the doors and under the chairs,
but she found no one.
Tom Thumb was hidden behind an envelope
on the rich man's desk.

Convinced at last that she had only been dreaming,
the housemaid blew out her candle and went back to bed.

Tom Thumb waited until the house was quiet.
Then he slipped down from the desk
and out through the window.
He made his way to the barn,
where he found a nice warm spot in the hay
and fell asleep.

When it was morning,
a milkmaid came to the barn
to feed and milk the cow.
The first bundle of hay
that she tossed into the cow's manger
was the bundle in which Tom Thumb was sleeping.

When Tom awakened,
he found himself in a cow's mouth,
about to be chomped by the teeth!

He tried to escape
but the cow's tongue pulled him back,
and Tom Thumb found himself on a long slide,
slipping down to the cow's stomach.
When he reached the bottom,
he looked around and said,
"My, it's dark down here.
When they made this place,
they forgot to put in a window."

In the meantime, the cow was eating hay,
and the hay was coming down the slide
into the stomach.
It was too crowded for poor Tom.
He called out,

"No more HAY, please! There's enough down here!"

Now, the milkmaid was seated on her milking stool,
milking the cow.
When she heard the cow speaking,
she became so excited that she fell off her stool
and spilled the bucket of milk.

The milkmaid ran to the house crying,
"Master! Master, come quickly!
The cow's gone crazy!
The cow is talking!"

"Not the cow, but you have lost your sense,"
said the rich man.
However, he followed the milkmaid
to the barn to see what was happening.
As they came through the door,
the cow was still saying,

No more HAY, please!
There's enough down here!

The rich man now thought the cow
was possessed by evil spirits,
and he ordered the cow killed.

279

The cow was slaughtered
and her stomach was thrown out on a dunghill.

Tom was just freeing himself from the stomach,
when out of the woods there came
a great, gray, hungry wolf.
With one gulp, he swallowed Tom Thumb!

Poor Tom! He was becoming discouraged.
Trouble seemed to follow him wherever he went!

Oh, Mr. Wolf! Are you hungry?

Yes, wolves and boys are always hungry.

"Then I can tell you where you can find
some tasty food," said Tom.
"Just follow the path through the woods
to the woodcutter's cottage.
Crawl through the drainpipe into the storeroom,
and there you'll find ham and cheese
and pickled eggs and smearcase
and spiced beets and boiled pigs' feet.
All of the good food that you could possibly want!"

The wolf didn't wait to be told twice
where to find a meal,
for his hunger was great.
He ran down the path through the woods
with his tail flying behind him
and Tom Thumb riding in his stomach.

281

When the wolf came to the woodcutter's cottage,
he did just as Tom had told him.
He crawled through the drainpipe to the storeroom
where he found all of the good food
that Tom had described.
The wolf ate and ate and ate . . .
and ate . . . and . . . ate.
At last he had his fill.

He turned back to the drainpipe to escape,
but alas! he had grown so fat

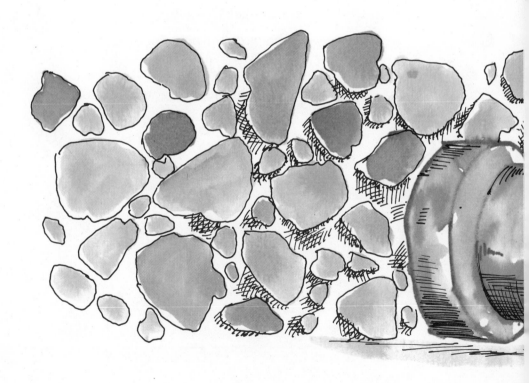

that he could not get out.

This was exactly what Tom Thumb had counted on!

Tom called out, "Father! Father! Come save me!
I'm home! I'm home! I'm home!"

Now Tom's voice didn't sound as loud
as you might think, because, remember,
Tom was inside of that wolf.
His voice sounded more like this:

Father! Father! Come save me!
I'm home! I'm home!
I'm home!

Fortunately, Tom's father was a light sleeper.

He heard Tom calling and he jumped out of bed.

His wife was right behind him.

They ran to the storeroom and opened the door.

When they saw the wolf,
the woodcutter grabbed an axe
and his wife grabbed a butcher knife.
Then they took after the wolf.

Oh, Father! Please be careful with that axe!
I'm inside of this thing!

Tom's father was careful, indeed.
With one well-placed blow of the axe,
he killed the wolf and Tom was rescued.

The woodcutter held Tom in the palm of his hand,
and said, "Welcome home, Tom!
Welcome home, son!"

Tom's mother was so happy that she began to cry.
"Tom, Tom," she cried, "where have you been?"

"Mother, I've been in a mousehole,
    I've been in a snail's shell,
    I've been in a cow's stomach,
and I've been inside of a wolf.
But from now on I'm going to be happy
just to stay home and sleep."

And that is exactly what Tom Thumb did.
He curled up in his mother's thimble
and he slept all of that morning
and half of that afternoon—
which is a long time for any boy to sleep.

Four Little Foxes

Speak gently, Spring, and make no sudden sound;
For in my windy valley, yesterday I found
New-born foxes squirming on the ground—
    Speak gently.

Walk softly, March, forbear the bitter blow;
Her feet within a trap, her blood upon the snow,
The four little foxes saw their mother go—
    Walk softly.

Go lightly, Spring, oh, give them no alarm;
When I covered them with boughs to shelter them
    from harm,
The thin blue foxes suckled at my arm—
    Go lightly.

Step softly, March, with your rampant hurricane;
Nuzzling one another, and whimpering with pain,
The new little foxes are shivering in the rain—
    Step softly.

by Lew Sarett